LIST

T0152096

MANUAL FOR DRAFT-AGE IMMIGRANTS TO CANADA

BY MARK SATIN
Director, Toronto Anti-Draft Programme

FIRST EDITION
First Printing, January, 1968 — 5,000 copies

SECOND EDITION
Second Printing, March, 1968 — 20,000 copies

THE TORONTO ANTI-DRAFT PROGRAMME

HOUSE OF ANANSI
TORONTO 1968

First published in 1968 by House of Anansi Press
This edition published in Canada in 2017 and the USA in 2017
by House of Anansi Press Inc.
www.houseofanansi.com

House of Anansi Press is committed to protecting our natural environment.
As part of our efforts, the interior of this book is printed on paper that contains
100% post-consumer recycled fibres, is acid-free, and is processed chlorine-free.

21 20 19 18 17   1 2 3 4 5

Library and Archives Canada Cataloguing in Publication

Satin, Mark Ivor, 1946–, author
Manual for draft-age immigrants to Canada / Mark Satin.

Issued in print and electronic formats.
ISBN 978-1-4870-0289-3 (softcover).—ISBN 978-1-4870-0290-9
(EPUB).—ISBN 978-1-4870-0291-6 (Kindle)

1. Emigration and immigration law—Canada—Popular
works. 2. Canada—Emigration and immigration—Handbooks,
manuals, etc. 3. Americans—Legal status, laws, etc.—Canada.
4. Draft resisters—Legal status, laws, etc.—Canada. 5. Vietnam
War, 1961-1975—Draft resisters—Canada. 6. Vietnam War,
1961-1975—Draft resisters—United States. 7. Canada—Description
and travel. I. Title.

KE4454.S28 2017   342.7108′2   C2017-901318-1
KF4483.I54C65 2017   C2017-901319-X

Library of Congress Control Number: 2017933808

Series design: Brian Morgan
Cover illustration: Sydney Smith
Typesetting: Alysia Shewchuk

Canada Council   Conseil des Arts
for the Arts   du Canada

ONTARIO ARTS COUNCIL
CONSEIL DES ARTS DE L'ONTARIO
an Ontario government agency
un organisme du gouvernement de l'Ontario

*We acknowledge for their financial support of our publishing program
the Canada Council for the Arts, the Ontario Arts Council, and the Government of
Canada through the Canada Book Fund.*

Printed and bound in Canada

RECYCLED
Paper made from
recycled material
FSC® C103567

MANUAL FOR DRAFT-AGE IMMIGRANTS TO CANADA

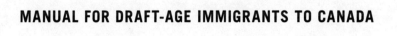

INTRODUCTION
"THE WELCOME MAT IS OUT IN CANADA"

BY JAMES LAXER

This manual, originally published by House of Anansi Press in 1968, tells of a time nearly half a century ago when Canadians were welcoming American draft dodgers and deserters to Canada. The United States was locked in the agony of the Vietnam War. The official toll of Americans who died in combat or of other causes in Vietnam is 58,220. While estimates vary widely, several million Vietnamese, civilians and military, perished. During the war, American society was wracked by the most severe divisions experienced since the Civil War.

The *Manual for Draft-Age Immigrants to Canada* introduced newcomers to Canadian society in a series of essays. Among the authors was J. M. S. Careless, the distinguished historian.

The manual summarized the workings of Canadian immigration regulations and procedures. The Canada to which those seeking refuge will be coming today has evolved considerably over the past five decades. Immigration laws have changed and as a consequence of the Charter of Rights and Freedoms, embedded in the new Canadian Constitution of 1982, the rights of individuals, including those of refugees seeking sanctuary, have been enhanced. However, a major barrier to the rights of refugees coming from the United States to Canada is the Safe Third Country Agreement between the two countries. The agreement deems the U.S. a safe haven for refugees and bars them from refugee status in Canada. With the Trump administration in office, that agreement is being vigorously challenged by human rights advocates in Canada.

In 2017, Canada is once again a refuge for people fleeing persecution in the U.S. A titanic societal struggle is underway inside the American republic, between a New America based mainly in increasingly multi-racial cities and an Old America centred in the South and the Midwest. With Donald Trump in the White House, Old America has come to power in all three branches of the American government. The Trump administration has lashed out at Native peoples, Mexicans, Central Americans, Muslim immigrants and refugees, women, the LGBTQ community, and trade unions.

The welcome mat is out in Canada. Evidence of this assertion is in the settling in Canada of forty thousand refugees from the Syrian conflict since November 2015 (as of January 2017). Enthusiastic Canadians have become private sponsors of a high proportion of the refugees. They have pledged themselves to support newcomer families during their first year in Canada.

Those who arrive in Canada from south of the border in coming months will find a country that is deceivingly similar to the U.S. As they will discover over time, it is also bafflingly dissimilar.

It's not that Canada boastfully proclaims itself a sanctuary for the suffering of the world. Quite the contrary, as Prime Minister Justin Trudeau declared in 2016, "Canada is a modest country." No Statue of Liberty welcomes the weary and the oppressed to Canadian shores.

History, geography, and culture have made Canadians skeptics about any notion of human perfectibility. Traditional conservatism is in the very bones of Canadians, along with a pronounced streak of social democracy. This makes even our liberalism odd, especially to Americans.

If you migrate to our country, you will find us welcoming and not very anxious to assimilate you. The term "un-Canadian" does not compute. Yet racism and exclusionism exist in Canada. When a horror occurs in Canada, such as the massacre of six Muslim worshippers in a mosque outside Quebec City in January 2017, Canadians condemn it in the strongest possible terms and proclaim appropriately that such an atrocity has no place in our peaceful country. The inclination of Canadians is to conclude that we live in an era in which xenophobic atrocities afflict humanity and that we have no special protection from them. Most Canadians are not inclined to believe that we can erect a "City on a Hill" in which perfection is within reach.

A major explanation for the oddness of the country is that the regions that are at the centre of today's transcontinental Canada were remnants left to Britain following the American Revolution. English-speaking Canadians are historically rooted in counter-revolution. Indeed, the Québécois are descended from the French-speaking people who avoided the French Revolution as a consequence of the British conquest of New France in 1759. For a century and a half following the Conquest, the most potent institution in French Canada was the Roman Catholic Church.

None of this is meant to suggest that Anglophones, Francophones, and the millions of Canadians who are descended from newcomers from many parts of the world are conservatives. Those who now occupy the lands of Aboriginal peoples, without having yet come close to recognizing the rights of those peoples, have created a country that is not rooted in a quasi-religious obeisance to the values of eighteenth-century Founders. Canadians draw heavily on their past — on the things Canadians have achieved together — without fearing the future to the extent that is so patently the case in the United States and in much of Europe.

Our history makes Canada uniquely suited to welcoming refugees in the era of Donald Trump and the alt-right, just as it has welcomed refugees in the past. The first African-Americans to be freed from slavery in substantial numbers were those liberated by the British military during the American Revolutionary War and the War of 1812. They found homes in British North America. Much better known, of course, was the Underground Railroad, a vast and heroic organizational undertaking within the United States that shepherded tens of thousands of escaped slaves across the North to freedom in Canada. A former slave herself, Harriet Tubman returned again and again to the South to lead men, women, and children to Canada. In a CBC broadcast in the 1960s, Martin Luther King drove home the point that the North Star was very important to slaves in the South. To the slaves, the North Star meant Canada, and freedom.

During America's wars, the war weary and those who refused to fight for what they saw as immoral causes deserted or escaped the draft by making their way to Canada. Best known among them were the thousands who migrated during the Vietnam War. I remember them well, met dozens of them, and count some of them as my friends to this day. Indeed, I wrote a section of the second edition of the *Manual*, published in 1968, on the kinds of colleges and universities Americans would find in Canada.

The Vietnam War was not the only conflict that drove many young men to seek sanctuary across the northern border. During the Civil War, thousands of soldiers, fighting in the armies of the North, deserted and fled to British North America. In fact, there was a two-way flow in those years. About forty thousand British North Americans migrated south to join the Union army, many drawn by the cause of fighting slavery, others hoping for adventure and a more exciting life. During the Iraq War, American deserters — the draft had been abolished — came North.

Today's refugees from Trump's America come from many cultures and countries. Some are from Middle Eastern countries, others are Hispanics, originally from Mexico or Central America. In the aftermath of the terror attacks on September 11, 2001, some Muslims came North in response to the repression and discrimination they experienced. There is nothing perfect about the Canada to which refugees come today. Despite the presence of bigots in the country, however, it is on the whole a tolerant, welcoming society.

Over time, newcomers will come to appreciate the vastness of Canada. In its forests, lakes, mountains, prairies, and incomparable rivers, they will discover a land that has been home to Aboriginal peoples for thousands of years. It is a land whose timeless character is an antidote to the feverish struggles of humanity in our time.

In 1936 Canada's great humourist Stephen Leacock wrote a reflective piece that captured the Canadian sense of place: "To all of us here, the vast unknown country of the North, reaching away to the polar seas, supplies a peculiar mental background. I like to think that in a few short hours in a train or car I can be in the primeval wilderness of the North."

One could do much worse than to live in Canada.

MANUAL FOR DRAFT-AGE IMMIGRANTS TO CANADA

All orders for the manual will be filled, no matter what the terms requested. We will sell on consignment, and we will sell at cost of paper and printing when necessary. But the Programme staff has to answer 100 letters per day and counsel 20 visitors, as well as myriad other duties, and the printer and Her Majesty's Mail must be paid in advance. We can not afford to subsidize any but the most struggling of peace groups. (We know all peace groups are struggling, but how would you like to be a New Left group in Georgia?) So we would request that all bulk orders (over 10) be paid for at a 40% discount, and as promptly as possible.

TABLE OF CONTENTS

PART TWO: CANADA

APPENDIX

NEW TO THE 2017 EDITION

TO THE UNDERGROUND RAILROAD
TORONTO, October 4th, 1853

Dear Sir: — I take this method of informing you that I am well, and that I got to this city all safe and sound, though I did not get here as soon as I expect.....

Nine months I was trying to get away. I was secreted for a long time in a kitchen of a merchant near the corner of Franklyn and 7th streets, at Richmond, where I was well taken care of, by a lady friend of my mother. When I got tired of staying in that place, I wrote myself a pass to pass myself to Petersburg.....

Sir I found this to be a very handsome city. I like it better than any city I ever saw. It are not as large as the city that you live in, but it is very large place much more so than I expect to find it. I seen the gentleman that you give me letter to. I think him much of a gentleman. I got into work on Monday.

Mr. Still, I have been looking and looking for my friends for several days, but have not seen nor heard of them. I hope and trust in the Lord Almighty that all things are well with them.

Believe me sir to be your well wisher.
John H. Hill.

TO THE TORONTO ANTI-DRAFT PROGRAMME
TORONTO, November 10, 1967

Dear Mark,

Just a note to tell you that we got in smoothly, and to thank you very much for everything.

You know we were almost apprehended by the FBI — my fault for staying so long. My girlfriend told everybody we were heading North, and right after my induction date two Agents came to my house and asked Mother where I was. She tried to keep them out, but they searched the house from top to bottom. I hid under some dirty clothes in the closet — thank God I wasn't all packed!

Toronto is just great. The people are less intense here, less ego-involved in world affairs. The streets are remarkably clean, and some of the subways even have rugs. The city grows on you. The job scene is better here than I expected. Jobwise it's like any prosperous American city.

The one thing I miss in Toronto is my friends, but most of them are coming up later.

Thank you once again for all you've done.

Peace and Love,
Dean

WORDS FROM CANADIANS.

"We Are Happy to Welcome You"
by VINCENT KELLY, L.L.B., Barrister and Solicitor

Even though circumstance and not choice has made Canada your haven, we are happy to welcome you. Those of us providing service to the Anti-Draft Programme assume that your opposition to the war in Vietnam stems from principle and therefore you are likely to become outstanding citizens.

Be forewarned that this opinion is not shared by Canadians generally. Our society is no less conservative, no less enthusiastic about containing Communism than yours.

If we had not burdened ourselves with participation as the Western representative on the International Control Commission (ICC), we would undoubtedly now be another Uncle Tom ally in South Vietnam.

Legally too our societies are similar. We adhere to most of the Anglo-Saxon precepts of natural justice but have no entrenched Bill of Rights. As a result, significant differences arise in connection with right to counsel and admission of illegally obtained evidence, to cite two instances.

But if you do enter our country legally and abide here peaceably the likelihood of deportation is remote. Deportation *is* probable if you become involved in criminal offences involving moral turpitude.

Entry is a straight-forward administrative matter. I am confident that the average young American could fulfill our legal requirements just as thousands of young English, Italian, French, and other foreign nationals do each year.

If there is any question concerning the immigration procedure which causes you concern, contact an anti-draft programme; if they cannot answer your problem they will put you in touch with competent legal counsel.

(Ed. note. Mr. Kelly himself can be reached at 85 Richmond Street West, Suite 701, Toronto 1, Ontario (416) 368-6464.)

"Discrimination Against Immigrants Is Strictly Prohibited"

by ROBERT D. KATZ, employment counsellor, Canada Manpower Division, Department of Manpower and Immigration

Although most Canadians agree that their government is in need of reform, they are also aware that Canada may well be the most functioning democracy in the world. Freedom of speech is not limited to the crackpot orator who will probably lose his job the next day. In Parliament issues actually are debated and the public has a fairly realistic view of why a bill has been passed or defeated.

There is little homogeneity among Canada's provinces. In New Brunswick or Quebec, for example, French is the dominant language. In British Columbia the cities seem more a part of Britain than North America. Even the climate is as miserable as England's. Then there are cities where an adult can live fifty years and never be required to know a word of English or French, cities where all the signs are in Russian, Hungarian, Italian or another European language. No attempt is made by the Government to force an integration of these cultures, and as a result an atmosphere of freedom prevails throughout Canada.

This has a strong influence on foreign policy. Although Canada is the second largest nation on earth it has never launched a war and seldom becomes involved in one.

To deny that discrimination exists in Canada would be to deny human nature, but it is so much more subdued here that an American will have trouble discovering it at first. Discrimination against immigrants is strictly prohibited. Most of the provinces have laws prohibiting discrimination on grounds of race, religion or natural origin. Many have strict prohibitions on age discrimination. I am not suggesting that every company in Canada will hire draft resisters, but most companies will.

(Ed. note. Here and in his two chapters, Mr. Katz is writing as a private individual and not as a spokesman for the Immigration Department.)

"Our Identity Is Up for Grabs"
by DR. WILLIAM E. MANN, *Professor of Sociology,*
Atkinson College, York University

Crossing the border to Canada is something like going to a slightly less mature version of certain parts of the United States. Originally Canada was dominated by Britain, by symbols of the Crown, Queen and Empire. Many Canadians have recently found themselves turning away from such reminders of colonial status. This is especially true of those under 40 and those in Quebec. Much of the thinking and attitudes of the younger generation have been shaped by the United States so the differences in speech, interests, and outlook are not clear.

As a people Canadians are, however, different, partly in their style and partly in their expectations. We are more inclined than Americans to conformity, to some lingering attachments to puritanism, to obeying the law, and to cautious investigation of new ideas. There is a certain reluctance to like the quite aggressive, the bold, boastful, or blatantly enterprising. Moderateness and a certain shyness are characteristic. Of course the styles differ a bit with regions: the Maritimers are more reticent and prouder of their heritage, the Westerners more outgoing and easygoing. Ontario is rather central both in geography and attitude. Quebec is fiercely independent, proud and emotional.

In expectations Canadians have less of the great optimism and less confidence in the future, but there is a lingering hope of some undefined but great destiny. In general expectations are moderate and plans made in business or elsewhere are restrained. There is a tendency to see Canada as facing a time of deep crisis, trying to find an appropriate place for Quebec and its aspirations, and trying to be independent and yet not lose the good things that American capital and enterprise bring us. Our identity in a sense is up for grabs.

3

by HEATHER DEAN, former staff member, Research, Information, and
Publications Project, Student Union for Peace Action

Every colony has its kept professors who train the natives to think of themselves as docile. It's funny to find Ted Mann in this role; he's rumoured to be a cool guy.

There's a concerted attempt to sell Canadians on the notion that the Americans own the country by default, not through the use and abuse of unequal power. For instance, Canadians who protest the steadily increasing foreign ownership of our resources are blamed for not investing in Canada. Nobody asks "With what?" but in fact the possible sources of investment — profits from existing industry, trusts, insurance companies — are not in Canadian hands. And, for instance, the U.S. threatened to have the Canada-U.S. auto-parts agreement defeated in the U.S. Senate if Time and the Reader's Digest were not made exempt from a bill designed to favour Canadian magazines. No Canadian initiative seems to be too petty to escape the club.

Canadians aren't afraid of losing "the good things that American capital and enterprise bring us" (who needs a stripped mine?), they're afraid of the Marines.

"Christians Are Called First to Love Rather Than Judge"

by the REV. ROY G. DE MARSH, Secretary, Board of Colleges,
United Church of Canada

From early childhood I recall stories of my maternal forebears who renounced their New England home and at great personal sacrifice came to live in Canada. History labels them United Empire Loyalists. The name implies fidelity to higher ideals than personal or family fortune, or the unquestioned support of the colony which aspired to sovereign nationhood through revolution. Freedom of dissent, whatever the cost, is a basic ingredient of the history of both Canada and the United States.

In vastly more complex and tragic circumstances today, Canada is again receiving a procession of people of a new generation who, in dissent from the Vietnam war policy of their nation, have made the often agonizing decision to leave the U.S.A. perhaps forever. In this informational guide no attempt is made to promote or discourage, to defend or attack the basis of that decision, or the ideals which are implied in making so painful a choice. The fact of that decision, and the value and autonomy of the person is accepted without question, and the booklet focuses most helpfully on the consequent procedures and provisions.

As a minister of the Church in the receiving country and having often said that Christians are called first to love rather than judge those who are in need, I find here a valuable example. Hopefully I urge all Canadians to reach out in the same spirit of this booklet, with concern and assistance to all facing the difficult transition to a new life. Some will need temporary accommodation or financial assistance, and help in finding employment. Many will suffer loneliness being away from family and friends. All will need friendship and acceptance. People of the Church I hope will be foremost in providing it.

ONE / INTRODUCTION
THIS IS YOUR HANDBOOK.

Slowly at first, and now in growing numbers, from Maine to Alabama to California, from ghettos, suburbs and schools, young Americans are coming to Canada to resist the draft.

There is no draft in Canada. The last time they tried it was World War Two, when tens of thousands of Canadians refused to register. Faded "Oppose Conscription" signs can still be seen along the Toronto waterfront. The mayor of Montreal was jailed for urging Canadians to resist — and was re-elected from jail. No one expects a draft again.

It's a different country, Canada.

"I didn't know where to begin. The Consulate tried to discourage me. I think they were prejudiced. The peace groups didn't know much. The hardest thing about immigrating is finding out how. . . ."

This is a handbook for draft resisters who have chosen to immigrate to Canada. Read it carefully, from cover to cover, and you will know how. It was written by Canada's major anti-draft programmes and their lawyers. Part One goes through the immigration process step by step. If you are still unclear, or face special difficulties that are not covered here, make sure to write. Or come in as a visitor and get help and advice.

Immigration is not the best choice for everyone and this pamphlet does not take sides. Four other alternatives are open to draft-age Americans: deferment, Conscientious Objector status, jail or the armed forces. The groups listed in Chapter 24 can help you choose among these alternatives or fight the Selective Service system as long as possible. Canada is not an easy way out; in many cases it means cutting yourself off from parents and friends. But there are many reasons draft resisters have chosen Canada — as many reasons as Americans. What these Americans are like is described at the end of Part Two.

"I thought I'd be chased out by the cops. Kidnapped! Or extradited. Or deported. Or something. . . ."

Canada has not "opened its borders" to young Americans. There is no political asylum. But an American's possible military obligations are not a factor in the decision to permit him to enter and remain. FBI agents on official business are barred from Canada. Most other Americans are welcome, unless they fall into one of the "prohibited classes" (see Chapter 16).

On April 12, 1967 General Mark Clark asked the Canadian Embassy in Washington to help return all the "draft dodgers." He was told that it would not be possible. Canada's extradition treaty with the U.S. lists the extraditable offenses one by one (see Appendix A); resisting the draft is not among them.

Americans can enter Canada as immigrants, visitors, or students (see Chapters 2-4) at any point in their induction proceedings.

"Well, you know, I can hardly believe this. I like it here. I thought Canada was the end of the world. Inferior schools. Inferior jobs. Igloos and log cabins everywhere. . . ."

You do not leave civilization behind when you cross the border. (In fact, many Canadians would claim that you enter it.) Part Two will tell you about Canada. We have not tried to sell you on Canada — our chapter on climate is chilling — but the truth is that Canada is a nice place to be. There is little discrimination by Canadians against draft resisters, and there is a surprising amount of sympathy. Most Americans lead the same lives in Canada they would have led in the U.S. Americans who immigrate are not just rejecting one society; they are adopting another. Is it really freer? Most draft resisters — and most Canadians — think so.

"But I can't go back home again, ever."

That's right. It can not be overstressed that draft resisters will probably never be able to return to the U.S. without risking arrest. This applies even to family emergencies. When a draft resister's father died last summer, two FBI agents showed up at the funeral.

Draft resisters have had and should continue to have only normal difficulties immigrating. Probably any young American can get in if he is really determined, though all will need adequate information and many may need personal counselling. We cannot emphasize too much that people should send us their questions or visit before they immigrate (see Chapter 25). Finally, the toughest problem a draft resister faces is not how to immigrate but whether he really wants to. And only you can answer that. For yourself.

That's what Nuremberg was all about.

* * *

FBI agents have told some parents that their sons can be returned. This is not true. Rumours have been circulated by U.S. authorities because there is no other way the government can keep young Americans from coming. One recent AP wire had it that 71 "fugitive warrants" had been issued for young Americans in Canada. The story implied that the warrants were valid in Canada. They were not; they cannot be. Unfortunately, some Canadian consulates are staffed partly by Americans and partly by Canadians who have been "Americanized." Draft-age Americans are often refused legitimate information and given incorrect versions of the law by these self-appointed recruitment officers. For example, some officials are telling young Americans that they can only apply through the consulates. Americans are very seldom told that they can apply at the border or from within Canada. One young New Yorker was told simply that "Canada doesn't want draft dodgers." It is a violation of Canadian law for an immigration or consulate official to give you false information to deter you from coming to Canada. Canadian anti-draft groups would appreciate receiving a notarized statement of such incidents. So would the Department of Immigration in Ottawa.

Public officials, amateur draft counsellors, lawyers who do not specialize in draft work, and, unfortunately, the "underground" press are notorious sources of misinformation. Read this handbook again and again, and contact a Canadian anti-draft programme if need be.

PART ONE

Applying

Rather than have war, I would give up everything.
I would give up my country.
— Hynmahtu Yalat-keht ("Chief Joseph")

TWO / LANDED IMMIGRANT STATUS
IMMIGRANT STATUS IS YOUR GOAL.

Americans who want to live in Canada must apply for landed immigrant status. A landed immigrant is anyone who has been lawfully admitted to Canada for permanent residence.

A landed immigrant can work, attend school, and in general carry on as any Canadian, except that he cannot vote in Canadian elections, cannot obtain a Canadian passport, and can be deported for a variety of well-defined offenses (see Chapter 15 and Appendix A).

A landed immigrant who has lived in Canada for any five out of any eight years is said to have acquired "domicile" and is eligible to apply for Canadian citizenship. Applying for citizenship is not a requirement but Canadian domicile is lost by a person "voluntarily residing out of Canada with the intention of making his permanent home out of Canada and not for a mere special or temporary purpose."

A landed immigrant is able to travel to other countries (see Chapter 18) or attend school or work elsewhere — temporarily — without losing his immigrant status. Time that an immigrant spends in residence outside Canada will not count towards domicile but will not jeopardize his immigrant status either. No time will be counted towards domicile that the immigrant spends in jail or in a mental hospital. Of course, it is best to lead a productive life as a landed immigrant, and going on welfare is grounds for deportation.

A landed immigrant is not expected to make periodic reports to the Canadian authorities; there is no "alien registration" as in the U.S. However, if you intend to leave the country for an extended period you might file a letter with Immigration assuring that you intend to return to Canada to reside permanently.

An immigrant's taxes should go to the government of the country in which the taxable income was earned.

American citizenship is not affected by landed immigrant status and the immigrant can return at any time. Even if a warrant has been issued for his arrest, Executive Order 11325 (1/30/67) will permit some disillusioned draft resisters to choose between jail and army service, at the discretion of the Director of Selective Service and the Attorney General.

An American who obtains landed immigrant status as a dependant of his parents will not lose his status if his parents return to the U.S.

Unless he renounces his citizenship an immigrant will remain a citizen of the U.S. until he obtains Canadian citizenship. It is not necessary for the immigrant to renounce until he becomes a Canadian citizen — and then it is a brief and automatic process. Obtaining Canadian citizenship is not difficult; see Chapter 19.

THREE / VISITOR STATUS
...BUT YOU CAN COME IN AS A VISITOR...

Almost any American can enter Canada easily as a visitor. People leaving the U.S. are questioned by Canadian immigration officials only, not by Americans. On the Canadian side an official will ask "Where were you born, where are you going, and for how long?" He may ask further questions, but the volume of visitors at most border crossings makes extensive interrogation impossible.

There are five factors here: physical appearance, money, duration of visit, plans, and means of transportation. Visitors with long hair, untidy dress, or peace buttons are detained more often than others. You should have enough money to cover however long you intend to stay. Most of the officials estimate that visitors need $10 a day. Further, even if the visitor does have money, the officers may suspect that he intends to stay permanently if he is vague or says he intends to stay more than a few days. Car is definitely the best means of transportation. Generally, train and bus are also acceptable, or, on the west coast, car, train, or ferry. Hitch-hiking and motorcycles are out. A round-trip ticket is good to have. Sometimes a visitor who is questioned more carefully will be given a card saying he can remain in Canada for a specific time period, not more than six months. Most visitors will not be issued a card. Names are seldom asked and almost never recorded. All visitors are expected to leave Canada within six months.

Generally a visitor will be asked to speak with a customs official who may want to make a cursory inspection of his luggage. Occasionally customs will go through the baggage — and vehicle — with extreme care. If the visitor has a car he will be issued a car permit good for not more than six months. If the visitor's car is loaded with household effects, the officer is bound to suspect his intentions. Americans who intend to visit Canada before immigrating should leave most of their baggage at home, or store it on the American side of the border.

Re-entering the U.S. is similar to entering Canada. Sometimes U.S. immigration officers will ask for draft cards, and enquire closely about your reasons for being in Canada. Canadian officials do not ask for draft cards, but a visitor won't help matters any by volunteering that he is going to see a committee to aid draft resisters or by mentioning individuals on these committees as if they were friends.

Visitors status permits nothing more than travel within Canada. If the visitor works or attends school he can be deported. Working papers can be obtained, but a job offer is needed first, and it is no more difficult to get landed immigrant status.

FOUR / STUDENT STATUS
...OR AS A STUDENT.

If, after consulting with a Canadian committee, you decide that landed immigrant status would be impossible to obtain, you might wish to apply for a "student entry certificate" (student status). Certificates are given on a year-to-year basis. At least two months' notice is preferred. Draft status is not a consideration, and students cannot be extradited for violating the Selective Service Act. Student status can be renewed from within Canada.

There are some disadvantages to student status:

1. In most cases you cannot get student status changed to landed immigrant status before graduation. Thus you would have to be fairly sure that you intended to finish school without interruption before you decided on student status.

2. Permission to work may be difficult to obtain. Work may have to be a complement to your studies. Thus you really would need outside support before choosing student status. Few scholarships are available to non-Canadians, especially at the undergraduate level.

There are three requirements for student status:

1. "Students must be of good character and without a criminal record." The applicant should appear earnest. A letter of recommendation from a former teacher might help. Students from Hawaii or Puerto Rico must furnish evidence that they are immune from smallpox.

2. "Evidence of acceptance" from a school. A letter will do.

3. "Evidence of sufficient funds for maintenance, full tuition and all other necessary expenses, including return transportation." This means funds for the whole year. Evidence can be in assets or a notarized letter of support from your parents. Possible earnings in Canada will not be considered.

Wives accompanying their student husbands are subject to the same requirements. But they will be issued "temporary entry" certificates, not student certificates. A student or his wife cannot work in Canada without written permission from an immigration officer. A student may be allowed to work part-time and summers so long as this does not interfere with his studies.

The "Student Application for Temporary Admission to Canada" can be obtained from the Consulates or by writing the Department of Immigration, Ottawa 2, Ontario. The application is not complicated; many of its questions (there are 20) repeat the ones on the immigrant form (see Chapter 7). These are the most important:

1. Proposed studies in Canada (attach letter of acceptance from university or institution): (a) name and address of school or institution in Canada; (b) if university, name and address of faculty or college; (c) course of study; (d) expected date of graduation.

2. Where do you propose to practice your profession, trade or craft after graduation?

3. Financial arrangements (indicate currency in terms of Canadian dollars): (a) Who is providing necessary funds, self or sponsor? (If shared, indicate approximate proportions.) (b) As proof of funds, attach: (i) bank statement showing available funds; (ii) foreign exchange control authorization to transfer funds; (iii) statement of sponsor concerning his ability and willingness to provide funds. (c) If you will be receiving any assistance from your government or other agency during your stay in Canada, please provide details.

4. Will you seek employment in Canada to assist in financing expenses? (give details).

5. Give names and addresses of references in Canada: name and address, relationship to you.

6. Will the references provide you with (a) accommodation; (b) financial assistance? (give details).

7. Family and dependents: give below particulars of your wife and children (whether living with you or not) and other dependents.

8. (a) If a dependent accompanies you to Canada will the dependent seek employment while in Canada? (b) Has employment been arranged for your dependent? If yes, give details.

Application can be made in four ways:

1. *By mail.* Application can be made to the Regional Director of Immigration nearest the student's destination. This takes considerable time.

2. *Through a Canadian consulate.*

3. *At the border.* The student can appear, with proper documentation, at the border and can be granted the certificate.

4. *From within Canada.* The student can enter as a visitor, gain admission to a Canadian school, and then apply for the certificate.

It is possible for a university student, like a visitor, to apply for permanent residence from within Canada (see Chapter Nine). However, it is necessary to declare an intended occupation and "student" or future plans are not acceptable. A number of Americans will enter Canada as landed immigrants with intended occupations, and then will decide to return to school. This is acceptable, and their status does not revert to "student".

The Canadian Service for Overseas Students, 388 Somerset Street West, Ottawa 4, Ontario helps students find lodging and friends. The foreign student advisor at your school can help in any dealings with the Immigration Department.

NEW LAWS WERE PASSED IN 1967...

On October 1, 1967 a series of new Immigration Regulations went into effect. The new Regulations spell out for the first time the principles involved in selecting immigrants.

Applicants now qualify for immigrant status if they can compile 50 of 100 "assessment units" based on their education, skills, personal qualities and six other factors, listed in Chapter 6.

"The main objectives of the new Regulations are to achieve universality and objectivity in the selection process," according to former Immigration Minister Jean Marchand. There had been complaints about prejudice from Asiatics and dark-skinned Europeans. It appears that the new Regulations have caused immigration officers to be more objective with draft resisters too.

Visitors are now allowed to apply for immigrant status from within Canada. (Formerly when applying from within, it could take a year to get permanent status.) "This innovation recognizes the growing ease of transportation," says Marchand. "In fact, a person visiting Canada to 'look things over' before making his final decision was penalized for this initiative." Applying from within is detailed in Chapter 9.

Students are also allowed to apply from within. "Foreign students studying at recognized Canadian institutions will be regarded as any other visitors applying for permanent residence," Marchand explains. It is, however, necessary to declare an intended occupation, and "student" is not acceptable. Post-graduate students or recent graduates are really the only ones affected. "Student status" is discussed in Chapter 4, Canadian universities in Chapters 34 and 35.

The ever-present rumour that "The borders are closing!" has lost all relevance. By including the provision for application from within Canada, the Immigration Department has shown that it is not out to "get draft dodgers." This does not, however, mean that application from within is the best way to get status.

The new Regulations provide for admission of three categories of immigrants: independent applicants, sponsored dependents, and nominated relatives. Only a relative can sponsor or nominate. How to apply with a relative in Canada (including a fiancée) is in Chapter 12.

Independent applicants can apply at the border, by mail, from within Canada or through a Consulate.

Applying is still not a "breeze" but there is greater fairness. As Marchand puts it, "Whereas in the past an individual could have been rejected on account of a single factor, such as lack of education, the new Regulations use a combination of factors in such a way that some of them may compensate for relatively low qualifications in other factors."

Eight of the factors are of an objective nature, and in a ninth the interviewing officers will take into account the personal qualities of the applicant. In addition, the applicant must comply with the basic requirements of good health and character established by the Immigration Act. He must not fall into any of the prohibited classes (see Chapter 16). And he must have enough money to ensure that he will not become a public charge in the event that he has difficulty finding a job, catches cold or something.

An immigration officer may approve an applicant who does not reach 50 units. He may refuse an applicant who earns more than 50 units "if in his opinion there are good reasons why those norms do not reflect the particular applicant's chances of establishing himself in Canada and those reasons have been submitted in writing to, and approved by, an officer of the Department designated by the Minister." This is not common.

A typical draft resister would start off with at least 27 points: 12 for his high school diploma, 10 for being under 35, and five for speaking English fluently.

SIX / THE UNIT SYSTEM
...MAKING IMMIGRATION A MORE OBJECTIVE PROCESS.

The nine crucial factors, and the units of assessment to be used, are reprinted here from Schedule A of the new Regulations — the official guide for immigration officers. Our commentary is in italics.

Try to estimate how many points you would obtain. Be conservative. If you do not reach 50, or if you want to "play it safe" — and we would recommend this — make sure to visit a Canadian organization helping draft resisters before you immigrate. They will help you find work (a job offer is worth 10 points) and will introduce you to Canadians willing to assist you (for question 14 on the application).

    a.   Education and training, 20 units maximum.

One unit for each successfully completed year of formal education and for each year of professional, vocational and formal trades training, or apprenticeship, up to a maximum of twenty. *A high school degree, then, is 12 units; a B.A. is 16. Half years do not count.*

    b.   Personal assessment, 15 units maximum.

Adaptability, motivation, initiative, resourcefulness, and other similar qualities to be assessed during an interview with the applicant by an immigration or visa officer, the total assessment up to a maximum of fifteen to reflect the latter's judgment of the personal suitability of the applicant and his family to become successfully established in Canada. *Usually these units are not calculated until last, and an immigration officer can use them to accept or reject a borderline case. Needless to say, be on your best behaviour. Married couples, especially with children, have an advantage here.*

    c.   Occupational demand, 15 units maximum.

On the basis of information gathered by the Department on employment opportunities in Canada, units to be assessed according to demand for the occupation the applicant will follow in Canada, ranging from fifteen when the demand is strong to zero when there is an over-supply in Canada of workers having the particular occupation of the applicant. *See Appendix B for a list of jobs in high national demand.*

    d.   Occupational skill, 10 units maximum.

To be assessed according to the highest skill possessed by the applicant, ranging from ten units for the professional to one unit for the unskilled, irrespective of the occupation the applicant will follow in Canada.

e.   Age, 10 units maximum.

Ten units if the applicant is between eighteen and thirty-five years of age, but one unit to be deducted for each year of age over thirty-five.

f.   Arranged employment, 10 units.

Ten units if the applicant has arranged definite employment in Canada which offers reasonable prospects of continuity. People who apply from within Canada are not given credit for a job offer.

g.   Knowledge of English and French, 10 units maximum.

    i.   Ten units if the applicant reads, writes, and speaks fluently both English and French;

    ii.   Five units if he reads, writes, and speaks fluently one of the two languages;

    iii.   Four units for each of the two languages he speaks fluently and reads well;

    iv.   Two units for each of the two languages he speaks fluently;

    v.   One unit for each of the two languages he speaks with difficulty;

    vi.   Two units for each of the languages he reads well;

    vii.   One unit for each of the two languages he reads with difficulty.

One year of high school French is better than nothing; mention it. Occasionally there is a short test.

h.   Relative, five units maximum.

Where the applicant has a relative in Canada willing to assist him in becoming established and eligible to sponsor or nominate him but is unprepared or unable to do so.

i. five units if the applicant's destination is the municipality in which that relative lives;

ii. three units if his destination is not the municipality in which that relative lives.

Eligible relatives are listed in Chapter 12.

i. Employment opportunities in the area of destination, 5 units maximum.

A maximum of five units if the applicant intends to go to an area in Canada where there is a very strong general demand for labour, fewer if the demand is less strong, and zero if there is an over-supply of labour in the area. *Destination units are subject to change. The major industrial cities of southern Ontario and the mining centres in the north rank consistently high.*

An independent applicant who intends to establish a business or retire in Canada may be given a credit of twenty-five units instead of being assessed for occupational demand and skill if:

a. he has sufficient financial resources to establish himself in business or retire; and

b. the immigration or visa officer is satisfied that any business the applicant proposes to establish has a reasonable chance of being successful.

Business experience is, of course, helpful here.

THERE IS ONE APPLICATION FORM.

There is only one application form. It is simple and short — like an application for college. Applications are available from the Consulates (see Chapter 21) or by mail from the Department of Immigration, Ottawa 2, Ontario. Prejudiced Consulates may be reluctant to give the form to applicants whom they know will be applying at the border.

The current application dates from October 1, 1967. Most of the questions paraphrase the old ones, but "Why do you wish to migrate?" has been dropped and so have questions on religion and ethnic origin. The first of these may come up in your interview.

Attach as many documents as you can to verify your statements. These might include:

a. a birth certificate or passport

b. a marriage certificate (if applicable)

c. high school and college transcripts (optional but especially helpful if you are citing specific courses you have taken as evidence of employability in a particular field)

d. school diploma (optional but important if degree more important than your work record)

e. apprenticeship or trade certificates (if applicable)

f. proof of any claims of money to be transferred later to Canada (e.g. a statement from your bank)

g. letters of recommendation from former employers (optional for immigration but important in seeking employment in Canada)

h. letters from former teachers (optional)

i. letters from adults who knew you (optional)

j. a letter for support from your parents if you are under 21 (very optional)

These letters might point out that you are a skilled and dedicated worker; that you adjust well to new situations; and that you will be given financial or other support if you need it. If you are under 21 you might include a letter from your parents stating that they know of your intention to immigrate and will be responsible for any debts you incur.

A letter is not legally binding unless signed by a notary. But it will help assure the immigration officer and may raise your "personal assessment" rating. You won't be asked for any of the "back-up" documentation; you should volunteer it when it seems relevant to the questioning. You might consider it insurance; it's probably not necessary, but a letter from his minister tipped the scales for one applicant.

Remember:

    a.   Answer the questions by printing in CAPITAL letters or by using a typewriter.

    b.   All questions must be answered. Reply n/a (not applicable) if the question does not apply to you.

    c.   If there is insufficient space on the form, answer on separate sheets, using the same numbers that appear on the application.

    d.   Children 18 and over must complete separate forms.

The questions on the form are reprinted here one by one. Commentary has been added in italics.

1.   My family name is, my first name is, my middle name is

2.   My sex is: male, female

3.   My present mailing address is

    This should be your last U.S. address, not a Canadian address.

4.   My telephone number is

    This should be your last U.S. number.

5.   Other names I have used or by which I have been known are (if married woman give maiden name)

6.   My date of birth was: day, month, year

7.   My place of birth was: city or town, province, country

8.   I am a citizen of

9.   If I were moving to Canada, I would:

    a.   take with me the following assets: cash (money), pension (transferable), other (specify), total value

b. leave behind to transfer later: cash (money), property-land, other (specify), total value

c. leave behind the following obligations or debts: person or company, total owing

Units are not given for assets but this is a major consideration. You should have enough to live on until you get established. Immigration's impression of you will be poor if you leave behind a great many debts. (Education loans won't count against you.) If you do have debts, you should be able to show that your assets are greater than your debts and/or that you have a steady job offer which will bring in enough money to pay them or at least a marketable skill. You might have documents that show how long you have to pay off the debt and what the payments will be.

In practice, $200 is sufficient for a debtless applicant with substantial job training or experience. $300 is a good minimum on the west coast. Naturally, the money that is necessary is related to one's job offer (how lucrative) or lack of job offer. $500 is generally sufficient for married couples, and $1000 or more will make it easier for a less-qualified applicant to immigrate.

10. My present occupation is

This should be your last U.S. occupation.

11. Intended occupation in Canada

Probably this is the most important question. Occupational demand counts for 15 points and the importance of your future plans cannot be overstressed. To get points for your intended occupation it must be credible. This means you should have a job offer if you intend to work in a skilled field in which you have no prior experience or training.

You are not supposed to apply for immigrant status if you intend to go to school in Canada. You will be asked to apply for "student status" instead; see Chapter Four.

If you use "teacher" as your intended occupation you will, as a rule on the west coast and occasionally elsewhere, be asked to clear your credentials with the provincial Board of Education. This can take months. Future teachers who present their credentials at the border are accepted

more quickly than applicants by mail. Especially in Ontario, future teachers with B.A.s who do not yet meet the teaching requirements may be accepted as substitute teachers (known in Canada as supply teachers).
This is for retired people.

12. I do not intend to work in Canada

13. I have a job arranged in Canada in writing; by word of mouth

A job offer is not a requirement, but counts for 10 units and helps assure the immigration officer you will settle down quickly. Remember that you are not allowed to start work before becoming a landed immigrant. There are other functions of a job offer, whether you are applying from within Canada (where offers don't count for units) or by mail or at the border (where they do).

a. *They prove to the officer that you actually have the skills you say you do;*

b. *They show good personal qualities: initiative, resourcefulness, etc.;*

c. *They make the money question somewhat less important since it is obvious that you won't run out of funds before finding a job.*

None of these can be figured precisely on a unit basis but they are all important. Most non-B.A.s, except those with training or apprentice-ships or solid experience in something skilled, should get job offers.

There are four important criteria for any job offer:

a. *The job should fit in with your past experience*

b. *The job should utilize your best skill. (In theory this doesn't make sense, since an unskilled but in-demand occupation should work just as well. However, in Vancouver and else-where, unskilled workers don't seem to be in demand, and unskilled jobs tend to be seasonal which brings up the next point.)*

c. *The job should be full-time, not transient or seasonal.*

d. *The job offer letter should clearly state that you will be hired after you receive landed immigrant status.*

Sometimes even a verbal job offer counts for 10 units if you can be specific. If you can't get a letter, know at least the name, address, and telephone number of your employer, your starting date and starting salary. Tell your employer that Immigration might phone to confirm the validity of the offer.

14. Should I go to Canada, the following person has offered to assist me after arrival (name and address)

   Only a relative will bring in units, but a friend's name will help. There are a number of sympathetic Canadians and former Americans willing to assist.

   A person willing to assist can increase the value of your application further by writing a letter of recommendation and support. His address can be your intended address if you make clear it is temporary.

15. Relationship to person listed in 14

16. My destination in Canada is: city or town, province

   Your area of destination is worth up to five units depending on how badly the area needs workers.

17. My present marital status is: single (never married), engaged, married, widowed, separated, divorced. Note: any change in marital status must be reported to the office handling your application.

   If you are divorced, a copy of the decree is required; if separated, a copy of the separation papers; if widowed, a copy of the death certificate. These requirements are strictly enforced and it is, in fact, occasionally difficult for someone who is separated to immigrate at all. There is a rationale behind this strictness. The Immigration Department doesn't want people running from their alimony or child support payments. A divorcé who had financial obligations towards wife or family might have evidence to prove that he had lived up to his financial obligations (e.g. cheque books).

18. The date and place of my marriage was: day, month, year, place

19. The name and address of my closest relative is

   Your parents unless deceased; this does not mean geographically closest.

20. Relationship

21. Country of his or her residence

22. If the answer to 21 is not Canada, the name, relationship and address of my nearest relative (if any) in Canada is

23. The names of my spouse, and children under 18 years of age are listed below: code, family names, given names, relationship, date of birth (day, month, year), city or town of birth, citizenship. In the Code Block — Mark "X" for those who will accompany you to Canada — "F" for those to follow later and — "A" for adopted children

   A wife (or fiancée) and children can help; their existence will assure the immigration officer that you will settle down and work. If your wife is qualified to work, or intends to work, by all means bring this up in a special note. And be specific. A wife's qualifications may give you personal assessment units which may put you over the line if you are not quite well enough qualified otherwise.

24. The full maiden name of my wife was

25. Family information

   a. Father's name, date of birth, city or town, and country of birth, present address in full (if deceased, give date)

   b. Mother's maiden name, date of birth, city or town, and country of birth, present address in full (if deceased, give date)

   c. Father-in-law's name, date of birth, city or town, and country of birth, present address in full (if deceased, give date)

   d. Mother-in-law' s maiden name, date of birth, city or town, and country of birth, present address in full (if deceased, give date)

26. Indicate what languages you speak, read, write (include your native language)

   English is worth up to five units and so is French. Do not overestimate your abilities, but do not underestimate them, either.

27. Education

Circle the number of years successfully completed in elementary school (1, 2, 3, 4, 5, 6, 7, 8); post elementary school (1, 2, 3, 4, 5, 6, 7, 8)

The details of my post elementary education are as follows: date (from, to), name and location of institution, type of institution, date certificate issued. I have successfully completed _____ years of formal apprenticeship in

_____.

Each year of education is worth one unit. So you should have eight years of elementary school. "Post elementary" refers to ninth grade and above. List your major if it fits in with your intended occupation or is background for it at all. Further, if you have had any vocational or technical courses, even in high school, these should be listed. The form doesn't have a place for this, so follow this sample on an addenda sheet:

date (from, to)	*name and location of institution*	*type of institution*	*date certificate issued*
Sept. '58–	*S.H. Rider High School*	*H.S. (two years work in drafting)*	*1962*
May '62	*Wichita Falls, Texas*		
Sept. '63–	*Midwestern University*	*College (major architecture)*	*n/a*
June '66	*Wichita Falls, Texas*		

All these details will have a bearing on what you can list as your intended occupation. Therefore they will affect your occupational demand and skill ratings and perhaps even your "personal assessment."

28. During the past 10 years I have lived at the following addresses:

If you have frequently moved about, you can give only your legal or mailing addresses. Instability is regarded as a bad sign.

29. During the past 10 years I have worked for the following employers: date (from, to), name and address of employer, occupation, monthly earnings (initial, final)

At least as important as your education is your employment record,

particularly if you do not have a B.A. or courses which qualify you for
specific employment. There is no better evidence that you are employ-
able. Of course, applicants in their early twenties are not expected to
have extensive work records, but they should have acquired some skills
and experience. Be sure to describe your job carefully to be credited with
the maximum skill ratings to which it entitles you; never say "factory
work" or "worked in a store." Especially, include any machinery or office
equipment you have learned how to operate. There is a great difference
between "construction" and "heavy machinery operator."

30. Since my 18th birthday I have been (or still am) a member of, or
    associated with, the following political, social, youth, student,
    and vocational organizations: date (from, to), name and address,
    type or organization, position held

    This question allows Canada to deport an immigrant who turns out to
    be a spy or saboteur; therefore they are freer to admit applicants from
    countries where it is extremely difficult to run a prior security check. It is
    definitely not aimed at American campus radicals. There is no Canadian
    equivalent of the Attorney General's list. Name any group of which you
    were "a card-carrying member" and describe it simply and uncontrover-
    sially, in one or two words. Of course, you should be prepared for hard
    questioning on the part of an individual immigration officer, but don't
    be intimidated by it; this is not grounds for refusing you.

31. Please answer the following questions by printing "yes" or "no." If
    the answer to any of them is "yes" give details on a separate sheet

    1. Do you have any physical disabilities?

       Anyone acceptable to the army would be acceptable to Immigra-
       tion. If there is something wrong with you, bring along a doctor's
       or employer's statement that this has not prevented and should not
       prevent you from being a productive citizen. The law is quite strict
       in prohibiting epileptics etc. — even when they are wives or other
       family members — and this cannot be taken care of by assurance
       of employability. (This may soon be changed.)

    2. Have you or has any of the persons included in this
       application ever —

a. suffered from mental illness?

Unless you can come out with an emphatic "no" here, your application will be in trouble. Unless your illness was long in the past, and you can bring forth proof you are cured — say, a letter from your doctor — you may not get in. It should be noted that visits to a psychiatrist are not mental illness. The mentally ill are hospitalized.

b. suffered from tuberculosis?

Ditto.

c. been convicted of, or admit to having committed, any crime or offense?

The same holds here. Bring court records and a letter from your parole officer. Even petty theft is grounds for refusal. In case of peace or civil rights offenses, check with a Canadian anti-draft programme, and be specific — was it "obstructing traffic", "resisting arrest" etc.?

The wording "admit to having committed" deserves comment. If you have committed, you do not have to admit to it, and this does not involve falsification.

d. been refused admission to or deported from Canada, or any other country?

Withdrawing your application does not constitute refusal. Anyone who has withdrawn should consult a Canadian committee before applying again.

e. been refused a visa to travel in another country?

f. resided in another country?

If you have never been a permanent resident (with papers) of a country other than the U.S. you have never "resided in another country."

g. applied previously for a Canadian visa?

This question is not for Americans. Americans never get visas to Canada and thus refusal of entry for any purpose is not refusal of a visa.

32. Individual passport sized photographs of yourself and your wife (if listed in 23) MUST be attached.

    A second passport photo should be obtained for your medical forms.

33. My personal description is: colour of hair, colour of eyes, height, weight. I have the following marks of identification

34. I wish to leave for Canada as soon as possible (check) or on (date)

    Border applicants should check "as soon as possible" — of course!

35. I understand that any false statements or concealment of a material fact may result in my permanent exclusion from Canada, and even though I should be admitted to Canada for permanent residence, a fraudulent entry on this application could be grounds for my prosecution and/or deportation.

Should my answers to question 17, 23 and 31 change at any time prior to my departure for Canada, I undertake to report such change and delay my departure until I have been informed in writing by the office dealing with my application, that I may proceed to Canada. . . .

(Date, signature of applicant)

Also you will be made to "solemnly declare" that your remarks are "truthful, complete and correct."

EIGHT / APPLYING AT THE BORDER
YOU CAN APPLY AT THE BORDER . . .

There are five advantages to applying at the border. First, this is the quickest method; a decision will be made on the spot. Second, an applicant who is turned back will probably be given an opportunity to withdraw his application; see Chapter 13. Third, a job offer counts for units at the border (as opposed to applying from within). Fourth, it is easier to get a job offer because you can come in and talk to potential employers just before you immigrate. Fifth, you would be dealing with less Americanized officers than at most Consulates.

There are two drawbacks. First, an applicant who appears at the border is going to be nervous and needs to be sure of what he will say. Second, a small but unrelenting few of the border officers may count your draft status against you; phone or write us for the current situation.

There is a possibility that Americans will eventually be discouraged from applying at the border, not because draft resisters are being discriminated against but because Consulates in the U.S. will be better equipped to handle them. *But the border is not closed now,* and any reports that it has closed should be promptly checked with us. Currently most Americans are applying at the border. These are the steps you would follow.

1. Obtain an immigration form and fill it out neatly and thoroughly. If you do not already have an application, the border official will give you one. But it is best to come prepared by getting one at a Consulate or by writing the Department of Immigration. This really is desirable. If you cannot, think out at least the answers to questions 27 (education), 28 (former addresses) and 29 (employment history) in advance.

2. The Immigration Department does not recommend that you take your medical examination until your application has been approved. At the border you will be instructed to take a medical in Canada within a few days. The medicals are usually administered and paid for by the Canadian Government.

    It is difficult to obtain a medical form from within the U.S. Some consular officials are prejudiced and will want you to apply by mail; they know time is on the side of the U.S. Government. Medical forms can possibly be had by mail from the Department of Immigration.

    The medical is expensive ($35 in New York City) and will load you down with documents. There will be chest X-rays several feet square, a radiologist's report, and Blood Wasserman and Urinalysis reports.

    Few border applicants bring their medicals along.

3. Obtain as many documents as you can, to punctuate your remarks. A list of relevant documents is at the beginning of Chapter Seven.

4. You should have a substantial amount of money with you — enough to live on until your first paycheque. See Chapter 7, question 9 for specific figures. Records of your assets should also be with you. Bankbooks are not acceptable; bank statements are. A letter from a bank manager testifying to your financial stability will be helpful if you are not bringing in much money or if your job qualifications are low.

5. If possible, your wife should accompany you and so should any children. Your wife, and children under 18, do not need to fill out separate forms; you will declare them as dependants.

   Few questions will be asked about your wife. If she is qualified to work, or intends to, by all means bring this up yourself. Often a wife's qualifications will be a deciding factor.

   Some draft resisters have moved to Canada with their parents. Whole families have been coming in recently. Your parents can return permanently to the U.S. without affecting your status.

6. Now you should be ready. Get a good night's sleep, bathe, shave, and get a haircut. You must appear neat. Applying for status is a suit-and-tie affair, even in 100-degree weather. The applicants who are most successful present themselves as good middle-class persons, determined to work hard and be a credit to their new country.

7. Driving up is best. A car is an asset, and indicates you led a stable and prosperous life back home. Being driven up is acceptable and so is entry by bus. On the west coast, though, entry by bus is not recommended for any but the most qualified people. In the east, entry by train is uncommon and thorny. Flying up sounds best, but there are retired army officers at the Toronto and Vancouver airports who will count your draft status against you.

If you visit Canada to get a job offer, you must return to the U.S. before you immigrate. Policy is different on the west coast. It is perfectly acceptable to say that you were in Vancouver looking for a job offer, that you found one, and then returned to the border. Also it is acceptable to come up to look around and decide whether or not you want to immigrate and happen upon a job offer in that process. Elsewhere, you should not give the impression you were in Canada minutes before. Otherwise, unfortunately, some immigration officers may suspect you were working illegally, or other devious things. At best you will be asked to apply from within.

It is not advisable to conceal that *at some point* you were in Canada. It helps, in fact, to point out that you had visited Canada to make up your mind about immigrating and to see whether jobs would be readily available.

8. You will not be stopped at the border until you reach the Canadian side; you will not deal with Americans at all. A Canadian customs officer will ask you a question meant for tourists. Your answer should be that you would like to apply for landed immigrant status. The officer will ask you to step inside the customs house for an interview.

9. The interview is not formal. Most applicants are nervous, though, and the tension will mount until you meet your immigration officer. Probably he is a family man who likes fishing and goes to church on Sunday. Try to feel at ease. If you appear uncomfortable or guilty, the officer (like anyone else) will become suspicious.

Often more than one officer will be involved, including a special inquiry or chief immigration officer who tends to be older and quite blunt.

The interview will take from half an hour to two hours, depending on how qualified you are and how many officers question you. If you have already filled out an application, the officer will ask you questions based on your answers. Otherwise the officer will ask you to fill one out right there, or will ask you the questions orally. Further questions will be asked, dealing usually with past employment, future plans, and reasons for coming to Canada.

The immigration officer has been instructed very bluntly by the Department that your draft status is not relevant to your application to enter Canada, and most will not ask about it directly. But they will frequently try to get at it indirectly by bearing down on your reasons for coming to Canada, and the way you handle this can be a major factor in your personal assessment. Remember, personal assessment is just that — *personal*. Don't pretend you never heard of Selective Service; the officer *knows* you're a draft dodger and this kind of coyness will only irritate him and convince him of your dishonesty. Be frank (stopping short of political or ethical sermons) and admit that you might not have considered emigrating except for the draft. But emphasize that your final decision was based — and it should be — on an appreciation of Canada and a determination to become a good citizen.

You should intend to work at once. If you have a job offer, you may be questioned closely about how you obtained it and what it would involve. Your employer may be phoned.

Another question might be whether you have any connection with Canadian groups to aid draft resisters. Such a connection is generally not an asset in the eyes of an immigration officer.

10. If you are accepted you will be given permission to work ("provisional status") and instructed to take your medical within Canada. Don't worry about the provisional nature of your status; mainly they want to check your chest X-rays for T.B. You may then proceed to your destination. If you are not accepted, you will be asked to return to the United States; see Chapter 13.

It may take several weeks for your final papers to reach you. Don't forget to leave a forwarding address until you get them.

...FROM WITHIN CANADA...

There are two advantages to applying from within Canada. First, Americans pursued by the draft will not have to wait for their papers in the U.S.; they can apply when they are safely in Canada. Second, applicants will be able to deal with immigration officers in person.

There are five disadvantages. First, applicants will not be given units for job offers (but a job offer will add to one's "personal assessment"). Second, an applicant who is rejected will probably not be permitted to re-apply. Third, the process is long (but not so long as by mail). Fourth, applicants may not be permitted to work until their applications have been formally approved. Fifth, more documents are needed than at the border or by mail.

Draft resisters will apply in somewhat this order. Our experience here is sketchy and there have been some individual variations. Of course, Immigration's experience here is also sketchy; applying from within is a new process, dating from October 1, 1967.

1. Enter Canada as a visitor.

2. Proceed to the office of a Canadian committee to aid draft resisters.

3. Proceed to one of the local immigration offices. Most Canadian cities have immigration offices, but it is probably speedier to apply at one of the five regional offices (see Chapter 21). The officers there tend to be better versed in the policies, explicit and implicit, of the Immigration Department.

   Tell the immigration officer you would like to apply for landed immigrant status. He will make an appointment with you. Appointments are made a few weeks, or months, in advance. Also he will give you two copies of the application form, one for yourself and one for your interview.

4. Fill the form out neatly and thoroughly. Include as many documents as you can, to punctuate your remarks. Sometimes

documents are especially important when you apply from within, and some applications have not been considered without certain documents. The Department of Immigration has issued this mimeographed form letter to some applicants:

Dear Sir or Madam:
.... To enable this Department to give further considera-
tion to your application, it is necessary that we receive...
the following documents:
- *School certificates issued by the administrator of all schools attended.*
- *Apprenticeship or trade certificates indicating the duration of your training and subjects studied.*
- *Your employment history since leaving school including references from employers, indicating your proficiency, type of work, period of employment and reasons for leaving.*

.... Your failure to comply with this request may necessitate the refusal of your application.

A list of relevant documents is at the beginning of Chapter 7.

5. Make sure to appear neat. Your interview will last longer than at the border and will cover more ground. Your background, skills, motives and plans will be gone into in depth. Remember that most immigration officers are quite human and will be interested in you as a person. Many of their questions, even on the draft, will be asked out of curiosity, or to gauge your reaction — not to "pin you down."

6. You will probably not be told whether you will be accepted. You will be asked for a Canadian address to which your papers can be sent. You will probably have to ask for permission to work while your application is pending. Receiving a paper for the Department of Manpower saying you can work while your status is pending is not automatic, as it seems to be at some border points.

7.   There will be a waiting period of six weeks to three months. Then (hopefully) a very noncommittal letter will arrive. Your application, it will say, has been "reviewed," and you will be instructed to take a medical, probably at an airport, and to mail in the results as soon as possible.

8.   There will be another, shorter waiting period until your medical is approved and your immigrant card sent off.

TEN / APPLYING BY MAIL
...BY MAIL FROM THE U.S....

There are four advantages to applying by mail. First, an applicant can continue studying or working in the U.S. while his forms are being processed. Second, a job offer would count for ten units by mail. (But the trouble involved in seeking a job offer for some time in the future and the necessity, in most cases, of a personal interview, makes this unwieldy.) A third advantage is that you can "get it all done beforehand" and can feel secure when the time comes to leave the U.S. Fourth, you don't have to go through the interview (unless consulate procedure becomes necessary) so there is less trauma.

There are four disadvantages. First, mail applications take a long time — two months to six or more. (At the Vancouver office, though, mail applications may only take six weeks.) Second, an applicant who is turned back will be officially rejected as opposed to unofficially turned down (see Chapter 13). Third, applicants who have received or are about to receive induction notices should probably not remain in the U.S. Fourth, there may not be a face-to-face interview, and without a chance to impress the officer with his personal qualities, a borderline applicant may not get in. Also, of course, it is more difficult to refuse an applicant to his face.

Americans who are not highly qualified or who have immediate draft problems should not attempt to apply by mail.

These are the steps an applicant would follow.

1. Obtain an application form from a Canadian consulate or Ottawa. Some Consulates may ask you for an interview. If not, or (in most cases) if your forms are sent from Ottawa, you will not deal with immigration officers in person. This is not necessarily to your advantage. "Personal assessment" counts for 15 units and it is difficult for a young applicant to convince an immigration officer of his "adaptability, motivation etc." on the basis of his application alone.

2. Fill the form out neatly and thoroughly, and send it, with as many documents as you can, to the regional immigration office in Canada nearest your intended destination (see Chapter 21). Documents are not required but will add weight to anything you say, and character references may add units to your "personal assessment" rating. These would appear to be especially important by mail. Documents also cut down on the length of time it takes to get an answer, since Immigration won't have to send you a note asking for transcripts, employment records and bank statements (occasionally they do).

3. There will be a waiting period of four weeks to two months or more while your application is being processed. 200,000 immigrants come to Canada yearly and to go over each application takes time.

4. A very noncommittal letter will arrive. Your application, it will say, has been "reviewed," and you will be instructed to take a medical (forms enclosed) and mail in the results as soon as possible. Medical forms will not be sent out unless your application has been found acceptable.

    The letter of rejection is short and to the point.

5. Have your medical forms filled out carefully. Do not try to shortcut any of the requirements. The X-rays really must be several feet square; the radiologist's report really must be attached. Otherwise you may be asked to take the medical again. Try to send your medical in promptly.

6. There will be another waiting period of four weeks to two months or more. Finally you will be sent a "Medical Certificate — Letter of Pre-Examination" which entitles you to immigrate. It is valid for six months only.

Technically you have not been accepted, but in fact you have, provided you appear at the border looking relatively solid and with the amount of money you said you would be bringing. At the entry point a doctor will review your letter of pre-examination and an immigration officer will fill out a final form, an abbreviated version of the landed immigrant application. But there will be no new questions. The officer will tear off a little white slip, sign it and stamp it and give it to you. From that point on you will be a legally landed immigrant.

*   *   *

It may become necessary for an applicant with draft problems to short-cut the mail procedure. The Toronto Anti-Draft Programme publishes a special leaflet for applicants who are drafted while their applications are pending. Draft-age Americans should cover their tracks by writing for it before they apply.

ELEVEN / APPLYING AT A CONSULATE
...AT A CANADIAN CONSULATE...

By late 1967 some Canadian consulates in the U.S. had begun to process landed immigrant application forms. Probably all the Consulates will be equipped to process applications by late 1968. Since this is a unique new way of applying, our knowledge of it is necessarily limited. At this point, so is that of the Immigration Department, but there are some inconsistencies. It appears as if the new method is here to stay, and if the border is ever instructed to refuse to process applications, the reason (the public one) will be that Consulates in the U.S. are better equipped to handle them.

From a draft resister's point of view, however, there are serious drawbacks to applying through a Consulate. Many of them are shared with the mail procedure (see Chapter 10) but one is unique. Applying through a Consulate takes three months or more, and an American who is draft-eligible may be inducted while his application is pending.

Officials at the Consulates who do not approve of draft resistance have not failed to take advantage of this. Several officials have misinformed draft-eligible Americans by telling them that it is not permissible to apply in any way other than through a Consulate. In fact, the Chicago consulate once issued a mimeographed form letter to this effect.

The advantages to applying through a Consulate are the same as applying by mail (again see Chapter 10).

Three things should be stressed here. First, most Canadian consular officials are objective and fair. It is entirely possible that you would *not* be discriminated against. But one prejudiced official can spoil a whole department. If you sense that your application is not being treated with objectivity, insist that it be withdrawn and/or contact a Canadian anti-draft group for further advice. Second, it is foolish to apply from within the U.S. if you face immediate draft problems. Third, if your draft problems are less immediate, and if it appears that you will earn *well over* 50 units (see Chapter 6), applying through a Consulate should not be ruled out.

* * *

Applying through a Consulate is simple enough. The applicant should inform the Consulate of his plans either in writing or in person and should ask for an interview. The applicant will probably be given two application forms before his interview (which may be set up for a month or more after he first contacts the Consulate) — one for his interviewing officer and one to keep for himself.

Advice already given about personal appearance, filling out the form etc., of course holds here too.

The interview is more or less similar to the interview at an immigration office within Canada (see Chapter Nine). The medical apparently must be taken within the U.S. The applicant will be instructed not to proceed to Canada until his forms have been given final approval.

. . . OR BY NOMINATION.

Americans with relatives in Canada can immigrate easily. Dependant relatives can be "sponsored"; others must be "nominated." Sponsored dependants would receive landed immigrant status virtually automatically. Nominated relatives must achieve 20 to 35 assessment units out of a possible 70. Almost any American would start out with a minimum of 23 points on this scale — 12 for his high school diploma, 10 for being under 35, and 1 (the minimum) for his skill.

Any landed immigrant or Canadian citizen can "sponsor" his

a.   husband or wife;

b.   fiancé or fiancée;

c.   unmarried son or daughter under 21;

d.   father, mother, grandfather, or grandmother over 60, or under 60 "if incapable of gainful employment or widowed";

e.   orphaned relative under 18; or

f.   adopted son or daughter (must have been adopted under 18; must be under 21 and unmarried).

The sponsor would apply on behalf of his relative. Sponsors can pick up the "Application for Admission to Canada of Sponsored Dependants" at any Consulate or immigration office. The form is one page long and in three parts. In part A the sponsor must give his name, address and occupation. In part B the sponsor must list the dependants he is sponsoring. In part C the sponsor must declare, "I understand it will be my responsibility when my dependant(s) arrive in Canada to provide for his/her/their accommodation, care and maintenance."

The application must be signed by the sponsor, his spouse (if applicable) and an immigration officer.

Sponsored dependants will not be questioned. Applications for a dependant relative will be accepted whether the dependant is in Canada or abroad and irrespective of the financial situation of the sponsor.

*   *   *

Any landed immigrant or Canadian citizen can "nominate" any of the following, including the immediate family of the following:

a. any son or daughter 21 or over;

b. any married son or daughter under 21;

c. any brother or sister;

d. father, mother, grandfather or grandmother under 60;

e. nephew, niece, uncle, aunt, grandson or granddaughter.

Every person nominating a relative for admission must "undertake to provide for a period of five years any necessary care and maintenance from his own resources for the nominated relative and his immediate family." Because of this the nominee will be assessed only on the first five selection factors. These are: education (20 units), personal qualities (15), occupational demand (15), occupational skill (10) and age (10); see Chapter 6. The other factors, according to a statement by former Immigration Minister Jean Marchand, "are of special relevance during one's first few months in Canada and are compensated for by the fact of nomination."

Depending on whether the nominator is a Canadian citizen or landed immigrant and the degree of family relationship to the nominee, the nominee must get from 20 to 35 assessment units (out of a maximum of 70). This is from Schedule B of the new Regulations:

1. A nominated relative must achieve

   a. *at least twenty units* in an assessment if that relative is

      i. a son or daughter 21 years of age or over,
      ii. a married son or daughter under 21,
      iii. a brother or sister,
      iv. the father, mother, grandfather or grandmother under 60, or
      v. an unmarried nephew or niece under 21 of a Canadian residing in Canada; and

   b. *at least twenty-five units* if he is a relative of a landed immigrant residing in Canada.

2. A nominated relative must achieve

    a. *at least thirty units* if that relative is

        i. a nephew or niece 21 years of age or over,

        ii. a married nephew or niece under 21, or

        iii. an uncle, aunt, grandson or granddaughter of a Canadian residing in Canada; and

    b. *at least thirty-five units* if he is a relative of a landed immigrant residing in Canada.

The nominator would apply like a sponsor, on behalf of his relative. Nominators can pick up the "Application for Admission to Canada of Nominated Relatives" at any Consulate or immigration office. The form is one page long and in three parts but is slightly more detailed than the form for sponsored dependants. In part A the nominator must give his name, address and occupation; he must also give his annual salary and say whether his relatives will reside in his home. In part B the nominator must list the relatives he is nominating. In part C the nominator must declare, "I understand it will be my responsibility to assist my relative(s) in his/her/their re-establishment in Canada and to provide accommodation, care and maintenance, if required....I assume the foregoing responsibilities for a period of five years."

The application must be signed by the sponsor, his spouse (if applicable), and an immigration officer.

Nominated relatives will not be interviewed, and application can be made whether the relative is in Canada or abroad.

THIRTEEN / RE-APPLYING
IF AT FIRST YOU DON'T SUCCEED, TRY AGAIN.

The great majority of young Americans are granted landed immigrant status on their first try. But if the applicant is not successful, all is not lost.

Very few applications are officially turned down. If the applicant wishes he can insist on an official decision and appeal if the decision is negative. This is not recommended. Appeals are rarely won and, if lost, the appellant will be ordered deported. He cannot re-enter after that for a number of years.

The alternative is more acceptable. The applicant should not object to being unofficially turned down or should offer to withdraw his application. He should then get in touch with us or with the Vancouver Committee to Aid American War Objectors.

FOURTEEN / EXTRADITION
TRY NOT TO GET KICKED OUT...

Extradition is the surrender by Canada to American authorities of a person who has been convicted or accused of committing certain crimes within the U.S.

There is a popular misconception that you can be extradited for any crime that is a crime in both Canada and the U.S. In fact, only the crimes listed in Appendix A are extraditable. Offenses connected with the Selective Service laws are not among them and will not be written into the treaties in the forseeable future.

An extradited person can only be tried for the crime stated in the request for extradition. U.S. authorities cannot lay charges against an American resident in Canada for, say, burglary (an extraditable offense), and then try him for infractions of the draft laws.

FIFTEEN / DEPORTATION
...OR SENT BACK.

Deportation is the procedure by which the Canadian government expels a person from Canada, usually to the country of his origin.

Any non-citizen, except a landed immigrant who has been in Canada for five years, can be deported for membership in a prohibited class at the time of his entry or if he has since become a member of such a class, or if he gained entry by fraudulent or improper means, including lying on any application form.

A visitor or student may also be deported for violation of the terms of his entry permit.

These points are worth noting:

1. A warrant in the U.S. for a non-extraditable offense is not grounds for deportation.

2. A landed immigrant who has been resident in Canada for five years but has not become a citizen is said to have acquired "domicile." A person with domicile can be deported only if he is found to be a member of a subversive organization or engages in subversive activities; he has been convicted of an offense involving disloyalty to the Queen; he has — outside Canada — engaged in activities detrimental to the security of Canada; or he has been convicted of certain offenses under the Narcotic Control Act, which defines marijuana as a narcotic.

3. A Canadian citizen, even a naturalized citizen, cannot be deported. At a deportation hearing the person being deported has a right to legal counsel. The decision can be appealed to an Appeal Board, and its decision may be reviewed by the Minister of Immigration. See the Immigration Appeal Board Act (1967).

A person about to be deported may be given the opportunity to leave voluntarily for another country.

There are few areas in which an individual's rights are more blatantly infringed than deportation proceedings. If you have trouble with Immigration, insist on getting a lawyer. A phone call to any of the anti-draft groups will get you one.

SIXTEEN / PROHIBITED CLASSES
THESE CAN'T TRY AT ALL...

People who fall into the following classes are prohibited from immigrating to Canada. Landed immigrants can be deported if they ever fall into one of these classes during their first five years in Canada. Naturalized Canadian citizens cannot be deported but can lose citizenship if obtained by misrepresentation.

Political Subversives. People who have been associated with organizations subversive to democratic government or persons "concerning whom there are reasonable grounds for believing they are likely to engage in or advocate subversion" are prohibited. So are "persons concerning whom there are reasonable grounds for believing they are likely to engage in espionage, sabotage or any other subversive activity directed against Canada or detrimental to the security of Canada." This does not necessarily mean Communists; the Party is legal, and conducts door-to-door campaigns here. Of course, an individual immigration officer might not be as objective as the law. But there is no reason to believe that anyone connected with American student radicalism would be refused on these grounds.

Drug users. "Persons who are engaged or are suspected on reasonable grounds of being likely to engage in any unlawful giving, using (etc.) in any substance that is a narcotic within the meaning of the Narcotic Control Act, or persons who at any time have been so engaged" are prohibited. In other words an applicant can be kept out, or kicked out, if an immigration officer even suspects him of using narcotics, including marijuana. Exceptions can be made if five years have passed since one was engaged in anything to do with narcotics.

Criminal offenders. "Persons who have been convicted of or admit having committed any crime involving moral turpitude" will not be admitted. The term "moral turpitude" is not defined, but one would suspect that it would involve any major crimes (U.S. felonies) but not misdemeanors or their Canadian equivalents. Of course, not all felonies would be crimes of moral turpitude, but one would almost certainly be prohibited with a felony conviction on the record.

There is a possibility that admission may be granted despite such a conviction if the applicant was convicted when he was under 21, and two years have passed since the completion of his sentence, or if the applicant was 21 or over, and five years have passed since the completion of his sentence.

In some U.S. jurisdictions a person can petition the authorities to have his records erased. Anyone with convictions which have not been erased should have his court records with him when making application.

Others. The Canadian Immigration Act prohibits immigration by prostitutes, homosexuals, mentally or physically defective individuals, chronic alcoholics, and persons "who are...or are likely to become public charges." This last consideration is extremely important.

With some exceptions, it seems unlikely that anyone would both be acceptable to the army and fall into a prohibited class. Anyone intending to immigrate who feels he may fall into one of these classes should check his situation with us or with Vancouver.

SEVENTEEN / MOBILITY
YOU'LL BE FREE TO TRAVEL...

Obtaining landed immigrant status is not illegal in itself and the landed immigrant who has not committed a draft offense is free to visit the U.S. — or to return there for good. However, it is possible (but in practice, not *yet* probable) that an American whose intent to avoid induction is known will be prosecuted for failure to keep his draft board informed of his address.

Americans who remain in Canada beyond their induction dates will be prosecuted. And it is foolish for draft-delinquent Americans to expect that they will ever be able to return to the U.S. legally. After you fail to report, the FBI, through the RCMP, may attempt to verify whether you intend to reside in Canada permanently. If you do, their investigation will be ended and a warrant issued. If you do not, the investigation may be continued — and a warrant issued. The U.S. has never granted amnesty to any of its war or draft exiles and there is no reason to believe that now will be any different.

Americans who obtain Canadian citizenship will be allowed to carry Canadian passports. Canadian passports will permit draft resisters to travel anywhere in the world, including countries "off limits" to Americans. But it should be noted that a landed immigrant who has not yet received his Canadian citizenship cannot carry a Canadian passport and should obtain an American passport if he hopes to travel outside Canada during his first five years. Landed immigrants from the U.S. are technically still citizens of the U.S. and it is perfectly acceptable for them to travel on a U.S. passport. Many do. The U.S.

passport expires in three years but it is easily renewable anywhere.

A United States citizen is not required to have a passport for travel to Canada or to Central or South America (except Cuba). A number of countries in this area, however, do require a visa. State and Federal Clerks of Court are authorized to accept passport applications, as well as the Passport Agencies in Boston, Chicago, Honolulu, Los Angeles, Miami, New Orleans, New York, Philadelphia, San Francisco, Seattle, and Washington, D.C. United States passports are not valid for travel to Cuba and "those portions of China, Korea, and Viet Nam under Communist control."

American draft offenders apparently can be extradited to the U.S. from Argentina, Chile, Colombia, the Dominican Republic, Ecuador, El Salvador, Guatemala, Honduras, Mexico, Nicaragua and Panama. (See U.S. Statutes, Volume 49, Page 3111. Some of the original signers have dropped out.) The Vancouver Committee to Aid American War Objectors is just about sure that draft resisters cannot be extradited from any other country for draft offenses, although they have not yet checked every extradition treaty. If you are planning to travel extensively abroad, make sure to cover your tracks by checking with them first.

It does not appear that young Americans are eligible for either the Canadian Certificate of Identity (a "stateless person's passport") or the Nansen Passport (issued by the U.N.). As a matter of policy, Canadian Certificates of Identity are not issued to Americans who have renounced citizenship, but only to persons who have lost citizenship involuntarily. They would certainly not be issued to someone who was still an American citizen. A recent U.S. Supreme Court decision has eliminated involuntary loss of U.S. citizenship. Thus travel on a Certificate of Identity is impossible.

Travel on the Nansen or U.N. passport is hopeless for the present. An inquiry to Geneva by the Canadian Friends Service Committee brought this response:

The Nansen passport... is granted to persons recognized as refugees, i.e., those who have left their own country and do not wish to return to it "through well-grounded fear of persecution on racial, religious or political grounds." ... I am afraid I very much doubt whether the High Commissioner's office in Canada would be prepared to recognize U.S. citizens who object to the Viet Nam war as eligible for refugee status. Do they, in fact, have "well-grounded fear of persecution" within the legal definition of this term? They may claim that they do, but I fear that the claim would be difficult to substantiate. In view of the generally-held opinion that the regime in the United States is as liberal as anyone could wish, I am afraid that dissatisfaction with a specific aspect of one's government's policy does not, of itself, constitute persecution.

EIGHTEEN / RENOUNCING CITIZENSHIP
...AND MAYBE YOU WANT TO GO BACK...

Renunciation of citizenship is not a requirement for landed immigrant status. But a number of Americans are wondering if they can escape indictment under the Selective Service Act by renouncing American citizenship before they have committed any violations of the Act. The only way this can be done is by obtaining a IV-C deferment from your local board.

Class IV-C contains "any registrant who is an alien and has departed from the U.S." If the registrant returns to the U.S. his classification is reopened, and if he was delinquent at the time of departure he is subject to arrest. There have been two questions in the minds of many U.S. draft counsellors concerning this possibility: whether the renunciation would be accepted, and whether someone who has renounced is an alien within the meaning of the Selective Service Act.

The Nationality Act answers these questions. Expatriation is a *right*. Congress has the right to decline to permit renunciation "in time of distress" but hasn't done so yet. The Attorney General has the power to refuse to accept the renunciation of a citizen "in time of war", but apparently only that of a citizen who renounces within the United States. And the Act states that someone who renounces shall be considered an alien and be subject to the laws of the United States as they apply to aliens.

We do not recommend renunciation. You should remember that you renounce the benefits as well as the obligations of American citizenship. The "laws of the U.S. as they apply to aliens" are not particularly benevolent. You would be able to enter the country as a tourist, but it is unlikely that you would ever be given a permit to work or study there. Applying to enter the country as an alien, you have no rights. People who have left the country during *time of war* to avoid military service are prohibited from re-entry. It would be a simple matter to extend this provision of entry requirements or to apply it to Viet Nam war evaders. And you cannot enter the U.S. as a stateless person; you must have a valid passport. This provision does not apply to Canadian citizens, but you will not have citizenship for five years.

It can be very awkward for you as a stateless person. You cannot travel. You will not have "domicile" in Canada for five years, and in that time you will be subject to deportation if you fall into a prohibited class. This could be something pretty trivial, like being a "found-in" at a party where someone has marijuana in his pocket.

If you are determined to renounce, you should have further legal advice on how to go about it. The process is outlined in U.S.C. 1501. There will be an investigation to determine whether you have a passport and it will be called in before your renunciation is accepted. You should also have competent advice on the exact form of your application to your draft board for a IV-C deferment .

(Note to draft counsellors and lawyers: for further research the relevant material is found in U.S.C. 1459, 1481, 1501, and, of course, the Selective Service Act, as well as the Canada Counsellor's Packet.)

NINETEEN / FROM IMMIGRANT TO CITIZEN
...BUT PLAN ON STAYING.

Recent amendments to the Canadian Citizenship Act have changed the requirements for Canadian citizenship. These are the new requirements:

1.   The applicant must have been admitted to Canada as a "landed immigrant."

2.   He must have resided in Canada five of the eight years immediately preceding his application for citizenship. The five years need not be continuous. Visitors and students living in Canada

before obtaining immigrant status may count half of each full year in Canada before obtaining immigrant status towards the residence qualification. The wife of a Canadian citizen needs only one year's residence in Canada.

3. The applicant must have resided in Canada for 12 of the 18 months immediately preceding his application.

4. He must be at least 21, or the spouse of and residing in Canada with a Canadian citizen.

5. He must be of good character and not under an order of deportation.

6. He must have an adequate knowledge of English or French unless he is the spouse, widow or widower of a Canadian citizen.

7. He must have an "adequate knowledge of the responsibilities and privileges of Canadian citizenship."

8. He must intend to have his place of domicile permanently in Canada.

9. He must intend to comply with the Oath of Allegiance:

I, John Doe, swear that I will be faithful and bear true allegiance to Her Majesty Queen Elizabeth the Second, her Heirs and Successors, according to law, and that I will faithfully observe the laws of Canada and fulfill my duties as a Canadian citizen.
So Help me God.

These steps lead to citizenship:

1. An applicant must apply on his own behalf.

2. Applications should be filed with a Court. Special Courts of Citizenship are in all the major cities.

   If an applicant does not live within the jurisdiction of one of these Courts, he may file with the nearest provincial court. If he lives more than 50 miles from a court, he may mail his application to the Registrar of Canadian Citizenship in Ottawa, who will file it with the appropriate Court.

3. An application filed with a Court must be posted for three months before it can be heard by the Court. Applications may be filed three months before the five-year period of residence elapses.

4. An applicant must appear personally for examination before the Court.

5. If his application is approved by the Court and the Secretary of State, he will be called before the Court to take the Oath of Allegiance, make a declaration of renunciation of his previous nationality in writing, and be presented with his certificate of citizenship.

A minor child does not automatically become a Canadian with the grant of citizenship to his parents. After one parent becomes a citizen the father may apply on behalf of his minor children.

TWENTY / CUSTOMS
THERE'S A LITTLE RED TAPE INVOLVED...

Americans can bring in or send up their possessions duty-free. There are customs houses at the border and within Canada. Duty-free possessions cannot be sold for 12 months.

CURRENCY EXCHANGE. The money system in Canada, as in the United States, is based on dollars and cents. But at the present rate of exchange, immigrants from the U.S. receive an 8% bonus when they convert their funds.

Immigrants are urged to exchange their funds at a bank, where they will receive the prevailing premium. Stores in Canada may give a lower rate of exchange.

POSTAL RATES. Canadian postage stamps must be used on all mail posted in Canada. Rates are slightly lower than in the U.S. Parcels posted in Canada for delivery to the U.S. must have a simple customs declaration attached.

BAGGAGE. The wearing apparel and "settler's effects" in use by the immigrant are admitted free of duty. Up to 50 cigars, 200 cigarettes, two pounds of tobacco and 40 ounces of alcoholic beverages, per adult, may be included. This does not apply to articles intended for other persons or for sale.

FURNITURE. An immigrant, or any person who obtains a residence in Canada, may bring in his household furniture and effects duty free. If brought in for temporary use, a deposit equal to the duty and taxes thereon may be required, and is refundable if the items are reported out within six months.

GIFTS. Gifts, excluding tobacco and alcoholic beverages may be allowed free entry if the total value of the gifts for any one recipient does not exceed $10.

FIREARMS. An immigrant (or visitor or student) does not need a federal permit to possess rifles, shotguns or fishing tackle in Canada. Admission of equipment, however, does not give the right to hunt or fish. Hunting and fishing are governed by provincial laws and licenses are required for each province. Regulations may be obtained from the Canadian Government Travel Bureau, Ottawa, Ontario.

VEHICLES. The entry of automobiles and trailers into Canada is a quick routine matter without payment of any duty or fee. Travellers Vehicles permits, good for up to six months, will be issued to visitors. Immigrants will not need permits. Motor Vehicle Registration forms, and copies of any rental contracts, are required.

Driver's licenses from any State are valid in Canada. An immigrant is expected to obtain a Canadian driver's license within 90 days. The driver's test is similar on all counts to State tests. Driver's handbooks are issued free by provincial departments of transport, and should be pored over; the laws are slightly different in Canada.

Unless an immigrant has the Registration forms to his car, it will have to be returned within a week.

CAR INSURANCE. United States motorists for their own protection may obtain from their insuring company a Canadian Non-Resident Inter-Province Motor Vehicle Liability Insurance Card. Possession of this Card indicates that the insurance company has agreed to abide by the minimum limits of Financial Responsibility prevailing in Canada.

An immigrant should find out if insurance is required in the province he is settling in. He will not be required to take out provincial insurance for 90 days.

FOOD AND GAS. Goods for consumption such as food and gasoline are dutiable, but "reasonable quantities" are granted free entry; for example, two days' food (per person) and gasoline up to the normal tank capacity of the vehicle. Motorists are reminded that the Imperial gallon is one-fifth larger than the U.S. gallon — which means fewer gallons are required to fill a tank in Canada, and gas is really not as expensive as it looks.

MEATS. Importation of uncertified meat shipments, weighing not more than 20 pounds, will be permitted provided the importer gives verbal assurance to customs that the meat is for his own personal use, and not for distribution or sale.

DOGS. Hunting and pet dogs may be brought in free of duty. Dogs must be accompanied by a certificate signed by a licensed veterinarian of Canada or the U.S. certifying that the dog has been vaccinated against rabies during the preceding 12 months.

CATS. There are no restrictions on the admission of cats into Canada.

OTHER PETS. Canaries and finches, other cage birds, monkeys, skunks, hamsters, guinea pigs, etc., are given entry into Canada without restrictions. Birds of the parrot family (parrots, love birds, budgies, etc.), not exceeding two in number and accompanied by the owner, may be admitted if found healthy and the owner certifies in writing that the birds have not been in contact with other birds of the parrot family and have been in his possession for 90 days immediately preceding transportation.

PLANTS. Immigrants may not bring in plants or certain plant material except in accordance with regulations under the Destructive Insect and Pest Act. Immigrants with plants are advised to write in advance to the Director, Plant Protection Division, Department of Agriculture, Ottawa.

EXPORT MOVEMENT. U.S. residents (including landed immigrants) returning from Canada may take back, once every 31 days, merchandise for personal or household use to the value of $100, free of United States duty and tax, providing they have remained in Canada 48 hours.

VISITING CANADA FOR LESS THAN 48 HOURS. Residents of the United States (including landed immigrants) visiting Canada for less than 48 hours may take back for personal use merchandise to the fair retail value of $10 free of U.S. duty and tax.

GIFTS. "Bona fide" gifts of articles other than alcoholic beverages or tobacco sent to a person in the United States will be valued at their retail value and will pass free of duty provided the aggregate value of such articles received by one person on one day does not exceed $10.

United States residents cannot bring into the U.S. certain goods of Cuban origin including Cuban cigars.

FOR FURTHER INFORMATION. Inquiries concerning admission of anything not covered here should be sent to the Customs and Excise Division, Department of National Revenue, Ottawa.

...BUT PLENTY OF PEOPLE CAN HELP YOU...

I. REGIONAL DEPARTMENTS OF IMMIGRATION

Americans who wish to apply by mail should write to the Department in the region of their intended destination. If you are thinking of settling outside these cities, you can get a complete list of immigration offices by writing to any Canadian consulate.

FOR THE MARITIMES: P.O. Box 129, Halifax, Nova Scotia
FOR QUEBEC: 305 Dorchester Boulevard West, Montreal
FOR ONTARIO: 480 University Avenue, Toronto
FOR THE PRAIRIE PROVINCES AND THE NORTHWEST TER-RITORIES: 83 Maple Street, Winnipeg 2, Manitoba
FOR BRITISH COLUMBIA AND THE YUKON: Foot of Burrard Street, Vancouver 1, British Columbia

II. CONSULATES

Canadian consulates are in the following U.S. cities (starred have Immigration Department personnel on their staffs):

Boston: 500 Boylston Street, (617) 262-3760
* **Chicago:** 310 South Michigan Avenue, Suite 2000, (312) 427-7926
Cleveland: Illuminating Building, 55 Public Square, (216) 861-1660
* **Denver:** 1575 Sherman Street, Suite 600, (303) 534-5123
Detroit: 1920 First Federal Building, 1001 Woodward Avenue, (313) WO. 5-2811
* **Los Angeles:** 510 West Sixth Street, Room 632, (413) 622-2233
New Orleans: International Trade Mart, Suite 2110, 2 Canal Street, (504) 525-2136
* **New York:** 680 Fifth Avenue, (212) JU 6-2400
Philadelphia: 3 Penn Center Plaza, (215) LO 3-5838
* **San Francisco:** 1 Maritime Plaza, (415) YU 1-2670
Seattle: 1308 Tower Building, Seventh Avenue and Olive Way, (206) MU 2-3515
Washington: D.C. (Embassy): 1746 Massachusetts Avenue, N.W., (202) DE 2-1011

III. TRAVEL BUREAUS

Canadian Government Travel Bureaus are in the following U.S. cities:

Boston, Massachusetts	New Orleans, Louisiana
Chicago, Illinois	New York, New York
Cleveland, Ohio	Philadelphia, Pennsylvania
Denver, Colorado	Rochester, New York
Detroit, Michigan	San Francisco, California
Los Angeles, California	Seattle, Washington
Minneapolis, Minnesota	Washington, D.C.

TWENTY-TWO / LITERATURE
...IN WRITING...

Following are some pamphlets, etc. on Canada and other draft alternatives. Americans who have not firmly decided on Canada should make sure to look into some of this.

CANADA

American Draft Exiles, by Robert Akakia. The House of Anansi Press, 671 Spadina Avenue, Toronto 4, Ontario. Available late 1968. $5.00; enclose 50 cents for postage. Draft exiles in Canada as seen by a philosopher and social critic. See Mr. Akakia's chapter on "current resisters" (Chapter 37)

Canada: 1867-1967. The Queen's Printer, Ottawa. $2.00; enclose 50 cents for postage. Magnificent 300-page book on Canadian life — in color

Canada Counsellor's Packet. Toronto, Anti-Draft Programme, 2279 Yonge Street, Suite 15, Toronto 12, Ontario. $5.00; postage prepaid. Includes the Immigration Act and Regulations, Marchand's speech in the new Regulations, the Citizenship Act, pamphlets on employment opportunities, special memos, and descriptive materials.

"Draft-Age Dilemma," by Olive Skene Johnson. *McCall's Magazine,* August, 1967. Best popular survey of new Canadians.

Draft-Dodger! A full-length LP by Todd Records, 62 Lakeview Avenue, Toronto 3, Ontario. $4.95; postage prepaid; Ontario residents add 5% sales tax. Eight draft resisters talk about why they came and how they find it.

"Emigration to Canada: Legal Notes for Draft Age Men." Central Committee for Conscientious Objectors (CCCO), 2016 Walnut Street, Philadelphia 19103. Free. Emigration and American law.

Ontario '67. Special Projects and Planning Branch, Department of Economics and Development, 950 Yonge Street, Toronto 5, Ontario. $1.00; enclose 50 cents for postage. Handsome collection of articles on Ontario by leading Canadian writers.

The Canadian Government Travel Bureau, Ottawa, has many descriptive pamphlets; you could also write the provincial travel bureau in any provincial capitol. Most cities have a Chamber of Commerce and many also maintain Tourist Information offices. Street addresses are not required for mail addressed to these offices.

OTHER DRAFT ALTERNATIVES

CO Counsellor's Packet. CCCO. $2.50. Includes CO Handbook and many important memos.

Draft Counsellor's Packet. Berkeley SDS Anti-Draft Union, 1703 Grove, Berkeley. 25 cents, Concise material on and against the draft.

"The Draft Law and Your Choices." Friends Peace Committee (Quakers), 1520 Race Street, Philadelphia 19102. Free. Conscientious objection and non-cooperation.

Draft Resistance Information Kit. Fellowship of Reconciliation (FOR), Box 271, Nyack, New York 10960. 50 cents. Includes articles, sample CO literature, and sample anti-draft flyers.

"Handbook for Conscientious Objectors." CCCO. $1.00. A must for every CO.

"It's Your Choice." FOR. Free. The draft and conscientious objection.

"The Non-Cooperator and the Draft." FOR. 5 cents. Why and hows of total non-cooperation.

"Our Fight is Here." Students for a Democratic Society, 1608 West Madison Street, Chicago 60612. 10 cents. Essays on draft resistance.

"Resistance to the Draft," by Stewart Meacham. FOR. 10 cents. Analysis of reasons for refusing military service.

"Up Tight With the Draft?" by David McReynolds. War Resisters League, 5 Beekman Street, New York 10038. 10 cents. Survey of draft alternatives from a pacifist perspective.

TWENTY-THREE / CANADIAN ANTI-DRAFT GROUPS
...IN CANADA...

Currently there are 26 anti-draft contacts in Canada. *Vancouver and Toronto are equipped to handle requests for information that is not in this pamphlet.* The others can help you settle down — with temporary housing, job tips, etc.

ALBERTA

Calgary Committee on War Immigrants, Station B. Box 3234, Calgary. (403) 243-5037.

Edmonton Committee to Aid American War Resisters. Box 322, University of Alberta, P.O., Edmonton. (403) 439-0478.

BRITISH COLUMBIA

Vancouver Committee to Aid American War Objectors, Box 4231, Vancouver 9. (604) 738-4612

Victoria Committee to Aid Draft Resisters, 1814 Oak Bay Avenue, Victoria.

MANITOBA

Dan Pentland, 194 Oak Street, Winnipeg 9. (204) 475-6851.

NEW BRUNSWICK

Fredericton: The Mobilization, P.O. Box 1582 or 130 Bailey Hall, University of New Brunswick, Fredericton. (506) 454-2428.

Moncton Area: Martha and Peter Kellman, 1379 Mountain Road, Apt. 4, Moncton.

New Brunswick Committee to Aid American War Objectors, P.O. Box 1355, Sackville.

NEWFOUNDLAND

Newfoundland Committee to Aid American War Objectors, Harvey Road P.O. Box 4174, St. John's.

NOVA SCOTIA

Nova Scotia Committee to Aid American War Objectors, 6124 Pepperell Street, Halifax.

ONTARIO

Guelph Anti-Draft Programme, 35 Fairview Boulevard, Guelph. (519) 822-4178.

Southern Ontario Committee on War Immigrants, Box 155, Station E. Hamilton, (416) 527-2857.

Kingston: Joan MacKenzie, 17 Parkwood Place, Kingston, (613) 544-1728.

Kitchener-Waterloo: Walter Klassen, 109 William Street West, Waterloo. (519) 745-4116.

London: Glen Tenpenny, 230 Platt's Lane, London. (519) 432-4718.

Oshawa Anti-Draft Programme c/o Stuart Roche, 302 Kingsdale Avenue, Oshawa. (416) 723-3474, ext. 13.

Ottawa: Mrs. Goldie Josephy, 2141 Rushton Road, Ottawa 13. (613) 728-3942.

Peterborough: Rev. Jim Allman, 581 Howden Avenue, Peterborough. (705) 742-5277.

Port Arthur-Fort William: Lakehead Committee to Aid American War Objectors, 162 Prospect Avenue, Port Arthur. (807) 344-8559.

St. Catharines: Dr. C. Owen, Dept. of Modern Languages, Brock University, St. Catharines.

Toronto Anti-Draft Programme, mailing address: P.O. Box 764, Adelaide Street Station, Toronto 2B; *street address:* 2279 Yonge Street, Suite 15, Toronto 12. (416) 481-0241. *American Immigrants Employment Service* c/o Naomi Wall, 921-1926.

Windsor: Information '68, P.O. Box 1233, Windsor. (519) 252-2052.

PRINCE EDWARD ISLAND

Teach-In Committee Against the War c/o George Robbins, Prince of Wales College, Charlottetown. (902) 892-3344.

QUEBEC

Montreal Council to Aid War Resisters, P.O. Box 231, Westmount Station 6, Montreal. (514) 931-3007.

SASKATCHEWAN

Regina: Dunc Blewett, 1200 Jubilee Street, Regina. (306) 536-2297.

Saskatoon: John Warnock Jr., Department of Economics and Political Science, University of Saskatchewan, Saskatoon. (306) 364-6590.

. . . AND IN THE U.S. TOO.

You should not decide on Canada until you've looked into the other draft alternatives. Following are the names and addresses of 100 contacts who can help you with them as well as with Canada. (Keep in mind that their addresses are not stable.) This is not a complete list, and you are invited to write us and find out which is closest to you. Most AFSC and SDS groups will give out draft information. The National Lawyers Guild and the ACLU will provide complete and inexpensive legal help.

TRAVELLERS FOR THE TORONTO ANTI-DRAFT PROGRAMME

C.J. Hinke, 123 Chambers Street, New York, New York 10007. (212) AL. 5-1341. *Currently working in the alternatives in draft-resistance: Canadian immigration and prison education*

Joe Taft, 1115 North 6½ Street, Terre Haute, Indiana 47807. (812) 235-2168.

GENERAL

American Friends Service Committee, 160 North 15th Street, Philadelphia, Pennsylvania 19102. (215) LO 3-9372.

Central Committee for Conscientious Objectors, 2016 Walnut Street, Philadelphia, Pennsylvania 19103. (215) LO 8-7971. *The best group for CO's.*

C.C.C.O. — West, 437 Market Street, San Francisco, California 94105. (415) 397-6917.

Draft Resistance Clearing House, 107 State Street, Madison, Wisconsin 53703. (608) 255-6575.

Fellowship of Reconciliation, Box 271, Nyack, New York 10960. (914) EL 8-4601.

National Lawyers Guild, 5 Beekman Street, New York, New York 10038. (212) CO 7-4592. *The best source of legal advice and aid.*

Students for a Democratic Society, 1608 West Madison Street, Room 206, Chicago, Illinois 60612. (312) 666-3874.

War Resisters League, 5 Beekman Street, 10th Floor, New York, New York 10038. (212) CO 7-4592.

War Resisters League, Joe Kearns, 5 Beekman Street, 10th Floor, New York, New York 10038. (212) CO 7-4592.

STATE-BY-STATE

ARIZONA

Jamie Newton, 5027 West Waite Place, Glendale 85301. (602) 937-8424.

Arizona Resistance, c/o Richard Dillon, P.O. Box 820, Tempe. (602) 967-8200.

ARKANSAS

Little Rock Draft Information Center, Mike Vogler, 512 East Ninth Street, Little Rock 72202. (501) FR 5-3544.

CALIFORNIA

Berkeley Draft Resistance, Steve Hamilton, 1514 Grant Street, Berkeley. (415) 849-4950 or 843-5222.

Berkeley SDS Anti-Draft Union, 1703 Grove, Berkeley 94709. (415) 845-2470.

Americans for Freedom, Bob Zimmerman, 1964 Vista Del Mar Avenue, Hollywood 90028. (413) 469-5495.

Los Angeles Draft Resistance Union, 1093 North Broxton, Room 238, Los Angeles 90024. (213) 473-6410 or 734-4745.

Ken Dursan, 1819½ F Street, Sacramento 95813. (916) 447-6456.

San Diego Draft Resistance Union, Don Sherman, 5055 University, San Diego 92105. (714) 281-8069.

The Resistance, Richard Harison c/o The Hearth, Howard Presbyterian Church, 1312 Oak Street, San Francisco. (415) 626-1910. *A major Christian resistance group.*

Brian King, 581 South 12th Street, San Jose 95112. (408) 287-6098.

Stanford Anti-Draft Union, John Saari, Box 2684, Stanford 94393.

COLORADO

Bruce Goldberg, 1077½ Lincoln Place, Boulder 80302. (303) 443-1926.

Colorado Resistance, P.O. Box 10453, Denver 80210. (303) 444-4682.

Sam Menor, 512 Polk Street, Pueblo 81005. (303) 544-1328.

CONNECTICUT

Rev. William Sloane Coffin, Chaplain, Yale University, New Haven 06511. (203) 562-7658.

New Haven Draft Information Center, 425 College Street, New Haven 06511. (203) 624-6657.

Connecticut Resistance Movement, c/o Richard Savage, P.O. Box 433, Storrs 06268.

DISTRICT OF COLUMBIA

Washington Draft Resistance Union, 1737 Q Street N.W., Washington 20009. (202) 667-6444.

FLORIDA

Alan Levin, Box 13636, University Station, Gainesville 32603. (904) 372-7227.

Jacksonville SCLS, Moses Davis, Box 1745, Jacksonville 32201. (904) 353-8933.

Miami Draft Resistance Union, Mike Meiselman, 940 Biarritz, Miami Beach 33141. (305) 864-3317.

Peace Center of Miami, 3556 Virginia Street, Room 202, Coconut Grove, 33133.

Tallahassee SDS, Pierre Musson, Box U-4594, Folirda State University, Tallahassee 32306.

GEORGIA

Atlanta Workshop in Nonviolence, Henry Bass, 1014 Piedmont Avenue N.E., Atlanta 30309. (404) 876-2159.

HAWAII

John D. Olsen, 2303 Maile Way, Honolulu 96822.

IDAHO

Ben Goddard, 2225 Division, Boise 83706. (208) 344-6077.

Campus Christian Ministry, Chad Boliek, 822 Elm Street, Moscow.

ILLINOIS

Chicago AFSC, 407 South Dearborn Street, Chicago 60605. (312) HA 7-2533.

Chicago Area Draft Resisters, (CADRE), 333 West North Avenue, Chicago 60610 (312) 664-6895; night, 493-8085. *One of the six "emergency" groups.*

Champaign-Urbana Draft Resistance Union, 1209 West Oregon Street, Urbana 61801. (217) 344-4483.

INDIANA

Indiana Anti-Draft Union, Janet White, 315 East Smith Avenue, Bloomington 47401. (812) 332-4569.

Purdue Peace Union, Mike Brand, 212-213 Arnold Drive West, Lafayette 47906. (317) 439-3611.

IOWA

Iowa State "We Won't Go," Don Siano c/o Physics Department, Iowa State University, Ames 50010. (515) 292-1168.

North Central AFSC, Leonard Tinker, 4211 Grand Avenue, Des Moines 50312. (515) 274-0453.

Iowa City Draft Resistance Union, Ross Peterson, 219 East Bloomington Street, Apt. 5, Iowa City 52240. (319) 338-6185.

KANSAS

David Leonard, 1137 Vermont Street, Lawrence 66044.

KENTUCKY

Roger Wook, 1130 Bardstown Road, Louisville 40204.

LOUISIANA

New Orleans Draft Resisters, Bob Head, 710 Ursuline Street, New Orleans 70016. (504) 523-4580.

MAINE

William Yerxa, 54 Graystone Park, Veazie (University of Maine).

MARYLAND

Allen Brick, 319 East 25th Street, Baltimore 21218.

MASSACHUSETTS

Boston Draft Resistance Group, 102 Columbia Street, Cambridge 02139. (617) 547-8260. *The major Eastern group and one of the "emergency" groups.*

Resist, 27 Stanhope Street, Boston. (617) 536-9793.

AFSC, 5 Longfellow Park, Cambridge. (617) 876-7939.

Draft Information Centre, 65½ Main Street, Worcester-01608. (617) 755-8170.

MICHIGAN

Michigan Area AFSC, 1222 Woodlawn Avenue, Ann Arbor 48104. (313) 665-3169.

The Resistance, Michael Badamo, Guild House, 702 Monroe Street, Ann Arbor 4810 (313) 769-0122.

Detroit Draft Resistance Committee, Box 9571, North End Station, Highland Park.

Detroit Draft Resistance Union, David Wheeler, 1172 Hancock Street, Apt. 35, Detroit 48201. (313) 831-6869.

Edward Lessin, 223½ Beal Street, East Lansing 48823. (517) 336-2259.

Owen Akers, Kanley Chapel, Western Michigan University, Kalamazoo. (616) 345-3958.

MINNESOTA

Twin Cities Draft Information Center. David Gutknecht, 1905 Third Avenue South, Minneapolis 55404. (612) 333-8471.

Alvin Currier, Student Union 213, Macalester College, St. Paul 55101. (612) 647-6296.

MISSISSIPPI

Freedom Information Service, Dave Doggett, Box 120, Tougaloo 39174. (601) 352-9788.

MISSOURI

Kansas City Resisters Union, T.E. Jepson, 409 East 54th Street, Kansas City 64110. (816) DE 3-4408.

The St. Louis Draft Resistance, Richard Freer, 5843 Cabanne, Suite E, St. Louis 63112. (314) 862-1925.

Washington University SDS, Suzy Chapple, Box 4685, St. Louis. (314) VO 4-0100, ext. 2413.

NEBRASKA

George Spangler, 633 South 14th Street, Lincoln 68508.

NEW HAMPSHIRE

James Newton, 307 North Hall, Dartmouth College, Hanover 03755.

New Hampshire Committee for Peace in Vietnam, Frederick Putnam, Lyme 03768. (603) 795-2206.

Putnam, Lyme 03768. (603) 795-2206.

AFSC – SANE Draft Counselling Service, 7 Park Street, Montclair 07042.

Princeton Draft Resister's Union, Doug Seaton, 48 University Place, Princeton 08540. (609) 452-7456.

Mrs. Daniel DeSole, Humanities 372, State University of New York, Albany 12203. (518) 438-4643.

Buffalo Resistance, c/o Larry Faulkner, 211 Ashland, Buffalo, 14222. (716) 884-9613.

Ithaca Selective Service Information Center, 306 North Aurora Street, Ithaca 14850. (607) 273-1932.

AFSC Draft Project, Mark Lyons, 15 Rutherford Place, New York 10003. (212) 777-4600.

New York Resistance, Lenny Brody, 5 Beekman Street, Room 1025, New York 10038. (212) RE 2-4272. *One of six "emergency" groups and among the most militant.*

Student Mobilization Committee, Gloria Ross, 17 East 17th Street, 4th Floor, New York 10003. (212) 255-1076.

Support-in-Action, C.J. Hinke, 224 West Fourth Street, New York 10014. (212) AL 5-1341.

Rochester Resistance, Box 5715, University of Rochester, Rochester 14627. (716) 235-0553.

Stony Brook Resistance, c/o David Gersh, Langmuir College, A-312 SUNY, Stony Brook 11790.

Owen Densmore, Department of Physics, Syracuse University, 102 Steele Hall, Syracuse 13210. (315) 472-1101.

NORTH CAROLINA

Robert Eaton, 452 Craige Street, Chapel Hill 27514. (919) 933-3566.

NORTH DAKOTA

G. Dean Zimmerman, 209 Fourth Street S.E. Valley City 58072.

OHIO

Cincinnati Draft Resistance Union, Bill Burge, 2323 Wheeler Street, Cincinnati 45219. (513) 421-9158.

Peacemakers, Dan Bromley, 10208 Sylvan Avenue, Cincinnati 45241. (513) 771-6485. *Marked pacifist orientation.*

Cleveland Draft Resistance Union, Tim Hall, 10616 Euclid Avenue, Room 317, Cleveland 44106. (216) 721-1869.

Ohio State Draft Resistance Union, Jim Buckley, 2299 Neil Avenue, Columbus 43201. (614) 291-3937.

Jim Custer, 413 Melrose, Toledo 43610.

Ohio Resistance, Antioch Union, Yellow Springs 45387. (513) 767-7843. *One of the six "emergency" groups.*

OKLAHOMA

Norman Draft Resistance Union, Joe Bateman, 530 West Eufaula Avenue, Norman 73069. (405) JE 6-8125.

OREGON

Henry Van Dyke, 3300 Van Buren, Corvallis 97330.

AFSC — Pacific Northwest, Jim Prall, 4312 S.E. Stark Street, Portland 97214. (503) 235-8954.

Portland Draft Resistance Union, Roger Lippman, 3203 S.E. Woodstock Boulevard, Portland 97202.

PENNSYLVANIA

Mr. and Mrs. Rick Allegeier, Samson Road, R65, Erie. (814) 864-8977.

Philadelphia Anti-Draft Union, Bob Dombrowski, 1515 South Street, Philadelphia 19146. (215) KI 6-6535.

Peace and Freedom Center, 5899 Ellsworth Avenue, Pittsburgh 15232. (412) 362-9000.

Penn State Freedom Union, Jim Grant, P.O. Box 923, State College 16801.

RHODE ISLAND

Suzanne Simon, 59 Helsey Street, Providence 02906. (401) 751-6818.

TENNESSEE

Southern Student Organizing Committee, 1703 Portland Avenue, Nashville 37212. (615) 291-3537.

TEXAS

Bill Langley, 1709 San Jacinto, Apt. 210, Austin 78705. (512) 477-2264.

Draft Information Center, c/o R.W. Foley, 4915 Swiss Avenue, Dallas 75214.

Houston SDS, Doug Bernhardt, 4141 Elgin Street, King Apartments, Houston 77004. (713) 748-6041.

VIRGINIA

Dennis R. Ciesielski, 1318 West 40th Street, Norfolk 23508.

Wylie Campbell Jr., 10 West Graham Road, Richmond 23222. (703) 648-5761.

WASHINGTON

Campus Christian Ministry, Lyle Selards, 530 North Garden Street, Bellingham. (206) 733-3400.

Seattle Draft Resistance Union, Mike Rubicz, 104 21st Avenue, Seattle 98122. (206) EA 9-2495.

Tacoma Draft Resistance, 2906 North 25th Street, Tacoma 98406.

Wisconsin Draft Resistance Union, Joe Chandler, 107 State Street, Madison 53703. (608) 255-6575. *The major Midwestern group.*

Milwaukee Draft Resistance Union, Jess Kleinert, 1012 North Third Street, Suite 210, Milwaukee 53203. (414) 273-6316.

LAWYERS

Ken Cloke, National Lawyers Guild, 5 Beekman Street, New York, New York, 10038. (212) CO 7-4592.

Edward Grogan, 2020 Milvia, Berkeley.

W. Edward Morgan, Suite 407, Tucson Tile Insurance Bldg., 45 West Pennington, Tucson 85701.

William G. Smith, Margolis and McTernan, 3175 West Sixth Street, Los Angeles, California 90005. (413) DU 5-6111.

EUROPE

We Won't Go c/o The Stop It Committee, 8 Rosslyn Hill, London N.W.3, England.

U.S. Campaign, Postfach 65, West Berlin 12, West Germany.

TWENTY-FIVE / QUESTIONS
LET US HEAR FROM YOU.

Now that you have read Part One carefully, you may have questions or you may want more specific advice on how to proceed. *Your chances of obtaining immigrant status will improve if you write us or the Vancouver Committee and include the following:*

1. Your draft status, and if and when you anticipate a change in status;

2. When you would be coming to Canada, where you hope to apply, and what means of transportation you would be using;

3. How much money you would be bringing — and how many debts;

4. Whether you think you might fall into a prohibited class (give the particulars);

5. Whether you have had any dealings with the Canadian Immigration Department (give the particulars).

We can tell you how you would fare in terms of units and recommend a course or courses of action, if you would include:

a. your age;

b. your intended occupation;

c. your work background;

d. your education and any occupational training;

e. your intended destination;

f. any relatives in Canada (and where they are);

g. the quality of your French.

PART TWO

Canada

I have been asserted to be wrong today . . .
I say my heart will never abandon the idea
of having a new island in the North.
— *Louis Riel, Canadian rebel*

TWENTY-SIX / HISTORY
YES, JOHN, THERE IS A CANADA.

by KENNETH MCNAUGHT, *Professor, Department of History,*
University of Toronto

I

Americans who know something of the history of their own country
will find both similarities and contrasts when they turn to examine the
history of the country to the north. Canada's history goes as far back
as American history, to the days of exploration and of first European
settlement in the 16th and 17th centuries. There is the long period of
colonial beginnings combined with an extensive experience in local self-
government, before full national independence is attained. In each case
states or provinces join together to form a federal union, and that union
extends its authority across the continent to reach the Pacific Ocean.
In each country the primary condition of national development is the
growth and improvement of transportation and other communications
facilities. Each country has a system of government based on representative institutions, regular elections contested by competing political
parties, and with free speech and a free press. Finally, each country

has faced the actual or threatened secession of one or more states or provinces, with the danger that the federal union would not survive.

But an American would also note numerous contrasts between Canadian and American history. Although Canada occupies even more of the geography of North America than does the United States, it has only one-tenth of the latter's population, and this disparity has generally been true throughout their histories. Moreover, Canada attained national independence by means of a gradual and peaceful process in contrast to the violent struggle which we remember as the War for American Independence. (Canada's first English-speaking population of any size consisted of refugees from that struggle — the Tories or Loyalists.) Thirdly, despite immigration from dozens of sources, the United States has developed as a predominantly English-speaking country, but in Canada one province — Quebec — has been predominantly French-speaking since about 1600 while the other provinces are predominantly English-speaking. Fourthly, the United States, through a policy successfully combining diplomacy and war, has become the dominant country in the western hemisphere and one of the world's super-powers while Canada's domestic history has been relatively unmarked by resort to arms and its role in the world has been, and is today, a relatively modest one. Finally, Americans have often thought that their country stood for something special in the world — a beacon of freedom, a haven for the oppressed, an experiment in republican government of the people, by the people, for the people; Canadians have usually been poor at coining phrases and they have never felt that they had a mission, a manifest destiny or a rendezvous with destiny.

II

Two themes deserve special emphasis: relations between French-speaking and English-speaking Canadians, and relations between Canada and the United States.

When New France fell to British arms in 1760, there were about 60,000 settlers along the St. Lawrence River from Quebec to Montreal, and with trifling exceptions all of them were French-speaking Roman Catholics. In the interests of peace and stability, the British conquerors did not disturb the institutions and customs which they found among the French Canadians, although they hoped and expected that the latter would eventually lose their language and religion. But such a change could occur only if there were a large influx of English-speaking settlers, and the latter did not occur. Years went by, and many French Canadians, especially in rural areas, never heard a word of English. Moreover, much of the population became increasingly self-conscious or nationalist in outlook, when it became clear that the British imperial authority did not intend to allow French Canadians to secure full control of their provincial government, executive and judicial as well as legislative. The upshot was the most considerable domestic insurrection in Canadian history, the Rebellion of 1837.

After 1837 there was a brief attempt to exclude French Canadians from participation in government, but it failed. Within ten years French Canadians were again politically active, but it soon became clear that they could not easily work in close political harmony with English-speaking Canadians. Government became deadlocked in the wrangles between the two groups. A way out was found in the Confederation of 1867, by which matters relating to education and religion — and property and civil rights generally — were assigned to the provinces, while the new federal government was to look after questions of common or general concern, particularly in the economic realm. The use of the French language was to be legal in the federal parliament and courts, and in the legislature and courts of Quebec, and the rights of the English-speaking minority in Quebec was also guaranteed.

Just as the expansion of the United States brought the slavery issue to a head in the 1840's and 1850's, so the expansion of Canada into the west and the participation of Canada in overseas wars led to dissension and controversy between the two language groups. Before 1914 French Canadians in the west were heavily outnumbered by English-speaking settlers and by immigrants from Europe. By this time earlier guarantees for the use of the French language in the West had been swept aside, and French Canadians became convinced that the use of their language was being restricted outside the "ghetto" or "reservation" of Quebec.

Moreover, from 1899 onward, the two groups were at loggerheads regarding overseas wars. Canada's participation in the Boer War, and above all, the imposition of conscription in the First and Second World Wars, appeared to French Canadians as brutal attempts by a majority to coerce a minority. To a considerable extent, French Canadians withdrew into a defensive shell, grimly determined to protect their language, their customs and institutions.

In recent years, and especially since 1960, French Canadians have begun to come out of this shell, to renovate their institutions, and to participate more fully in the modern, industrial world. But they are no less determined than before to protect their language against pressures, either from English-speaking Canada or from the United States.

III

Today Canada and the United States are friendly neighbours in North America, sharing the famous "4000 miles of undefended border" and looking back to 150 years of peaceful relations. It is nevertheless a fact that a large part of Canadian history has to do with hostility, apprehension, and suspicion directed toward the United States. It has sometimes seemed that the only thing holding Canadians together was a common dislike of the United States.

In the realm of war and diplomacy, the record of hostility goes back to the earliest time when French and English colonists burned each other's houses or egged on the Indians to do the work for them. American independence was preceded by an invasion of Canada in 1775-76. The War of 1812 saw several further attempts to invade and conquer Canada. At the end of the 1830's and during and after the American Civil War of the 1860's the border was the scene of tension and there was frequent talk of war. Canadians feared American Manifest Destiny, and maintained close ties with Great Britain as a form of protection. Until the end of the 1860's, the border was fortified and patrolled, not undefended. Since that time, the United States has been too powerful to make it feasible for Canada to rely on military defense, and in any event it was not in the interest of the United States to undertake a military invasion. But Canadians continued to worry about American pressures of various kinds.

In economic affairs Canadian national policy was based on a protective tariff, to keep out American manufactured goods and to build up Canadian secondary industries. It was hoped that an east-west economy would arise, in which trade with the United States would be kept to a minimum. But the protective tariff boomeranged. American companies built branch plants in Canada, and since the 1920's American investment in Canada has steadily grown. What to do about American financial control of the Canadian economy has become a leading issue in Canadian public life. The two economies are now so closely meshed that Canada cannot avoid association (some call it "complicity") with American enterprises such as the Vietnam war without bringing on mass unemployment. A further source of frustration is the fact that the Canadian standard of living has as a rule been about 25 per cent below the American: the only way to catch up is to sell more finished goods in the rich American market — and that means "complicity".

Finally Canadians have traditionally feared cultural and social pressures coming from the United States. As long as the ties with Britain were close, Canadians could try — with limited success — to combat these pressures by looking to British models with respect to education, literature, entertainment, and patriotism and loyalty. But to many Canadians such an attitude seemed to be immature or colonial, and it has nearly disappeared in the last generation. It is, however, not so easy to know what to put in its place. The problem has been sharpened by the enormous expansion of the mass media, especially television. The invasion is more peaceful than those of 1775 or 1812, but it may also prove to be more successful.

TWENTY-SEVEN / POLITICS
IT HAS POLITICS . . .
by HEATHER DEAN, former staff member, Student Union for Peace Action

I. INSTITUTIONS

The Canadian constitution, written in 1867, was concerned with two major problems: how to avoid anything like the American civil war and what to do about the French. The constitution was designed to give the Federal government much more power than its American counterpart; the provinces were given minor responsibilities like education and social welfare, and minor revenue sources like income taxes. Obviously, the course of history has caused a few changes unforeseen by Canada's founding fathers. The Federal government has rectified one error by borrowing the right to tax income during World War II and refusing to give it back, but in general the provinces have as much autonomy as they have money to take advantage of.

Provincial and federal politics are very separate. The political parties have independent organizations and provinces frequently vote solidly for one party in provincial elections and solidly for a different party federally.

"What to do about the French" is still with us. After conquering the French, our British forbears confidently expected that they would be assimilated in a few years. However the French did not disappear and English Canadians are still sputtering with indignation. The French in Canada have been almost an internal colony, taxed and legislated by a non-French government, their businesses and resources owned and managed by non-French. The Quebec government was traditionally corrupt, inefficient, repressive, and serviced English Canadian rather than French Canadian interests.

The most exciting thing happening in Canada has been "the Quiet Revolution" in Quebec over the last ten years. The new liberal government in Quebec has at least as honest a claim to the title "social democratic" as does the NDP, and is responding to even more dynamic social forces. Intellectual life, the arts, minority politics have all been transformed in Quebec, and if they do not gain freedom within Canada's existing political structures there is a real possibility of Quebec separating from Canada.

English Canadians argue that individually English and French Canada can not resist the encroachments of the United States. The Quebecois retort that they haven't noticed any "Anglo's" resisting terribly hard lately, and that, far from helping them resist the U.S., the English are dragging them down the drain.

Quebec is where it's happening, but the Quiet Revolution is fiercely nationalistic and an American couldn't make it there without impeccable (and non-Parisian) French and a great deal of cultural humility.

*   *   *

The federal government is composed of the House of Commons and the Senate. The Senate serves two functions: its appointees can be drawn from out-of-the-way areas and politically unrepresented groups (women, Indians, etc.) thus lending an impression of balance to the government; and it provides a generous retirement pension for party workhorses or people who need buying off. It need not be mentioned again.

The House of Commons, as the name suggests, represents an invasion of government by the British lower classes. Canadian school kids study the several centuries of erosion of the power of the crown and aristocracy by the British bourgeoisie (peasant and working-class representation was a late invention — the Commons weren't meant to be *that* common). Since the crucial issue of political power for several centuries was control of taxes ("no taxation without representation" was a *14th century* slogan) they get some grounding in the concrete determinants of power. But not much.

All legislative power is in the hands of the House of Commons. Members are elected from geographic areas of approximately equal populations, although the universal rural-urban shift creates some rural over-representation. The Prime Minister is the leader of the party with the largest number of seats; he is not elected directly. The P.M. appoints a cabinet which (with the civil service) is the executive body of the country and draws up legislation. If legislation presented by the government is defeated, the government falls. Therefore voting does not cross party lines. Since the party with the largest number of seats need not have a majority it could theoretically be overthrown immediately by a coalition of the smaller parties. But Canadians would consider this terribly unsporting and vote accordingly, so minority governments have been able in practice to rule as if they had majorities.

The government is elected for up to five years, so the party in power chooses the time that it will resign and fight an election.

*   *   *

The Queen is represented in Canada by the Governor General. He launches ships and debutantes.

II. POLITICAL PHILOSOPHY

Just as in the U.S., Canadians entertain three basic concepts of their political institutions; just as in the U.S. they are never taught these concepts, are usually unaware that they have them, and thus are generally observed to believe all of them at once. In increasing order of contemporary significance these are the free enterprise model, the representative model and the meritocratic model.

The free enterprise model. With six major parties, Canadians cross party lines to vote much more frequently than Americans, and this model has only recently been abandoned by the last of its faithful, the NDP. According to this model, the voter is selecting his choice of a number of *programs* or *platforms* advanced by various parties; the salesmen for the program that meets the needs of the greatest number of consumers win the largest vote and run the country, until a new improved product by a rival party captures the market. White's *The Making of the President: 1960* had as much impact on the bright young men in Canadian smoke-filled rooms as it did everywhere else, and you will not find a consistent platform in the campaign literature of any of the major parties.

The politician as representative. This hangover from frontier days still is reflected in a certain amount of ethnic and regional sleight-of-hand in the make-up of the cabinet and publicization of candidates. That small part of the population that voted before the Great War still entertains the idea that the member of parliament from their district should be a local boy made good; Catholics run in Catholic areas, and the Liberal Party was very embarrassed by the lack of a Prairie representative to appoint Minister of Agriculture. However, no Canadian would tell you that his government is composed of a representative sampling of ordinary citizens, nor argue that it should be.

Meritocracy. Generally, the young Canadian voter feels that he votes for "the best man for the job" and is rather smug about the ease with which he crosses party lines. He considers the Men In Ottawa to be the most competent, intelligent and best informed of the selections offered the voters. He does not see politics as a conflict between the representatives of different interests, nor as representative democracy in the populist sense. Where he votes "on the issues" the issues he has in mind are generally symbolic rather than concrete. He leaves it to The Experts. He suspects that the experts are fools. He shrugs.

III. THE PARTIES

The Canadian political spectrum covers everything from centre-right Republican to the left wing of the ADA. The drought and depression on the prairies gave rise to the same kind of radical populist movements in Canada as they did in the States, but in Canada these movements were not totally absorbed by the major parties and created a right and a left party that are still major forces in Canadian politics.

Social Credit. The Socreds have a stranglehold on the provincial governments of British Columbia and Alberta. The Alberta government is probably the crudest of the two, but both are in a race with the right-wing Liberal administration of Saskatchewan to see who can sell the country to the U.S. the fastest. The Socreds have never been a force in federal politics and never will be. Besides it depresses me to write about them.

New Democratic Party. The depression populist strain in Canadian politics centred in the Cooperative Commonwealth Federation. The CCF governed Saskatchewan for 20 years. Its most notable policies were strong encouragement of agricultural and consumers' cooperatives and the belated introduction of socialized medicine. (Incidentally, medicare appeared to raise the annual income of Saskatchewan doctors several thousand dollars per year. This oddity probably represents the average amount they cheated on their income tax returns.) The CCF came close to winning the post-war elections but has had to settle for chronic third-party status since then. It reconstituted itself as the New Democratic Party (NDP) around 1960 with much fanfare, attempting to forge a farm-labour alliance and to carry the left wing of the Liberal party along with the Liberal intellectuals who bolted at the time.

It didn't. The UAW and Steelworkers form the basis of NDP financing and support. Most of its federal members are elected from B.C., the industrial cities of southern Ontario — Toronto, Hamilton, Oshawa — with substantial strength in the mining areas in the north. Its future depends on a major breakthrough in Quebec, which is a realistic hope.

Most of the avowed socialists in the party are aging veterans. Its current motifs are integrity, competence, and modernity. "Image" is the in-word. Its founders are spinning in their graves.

The NDP has a vigorous youth movement that supplies most of the bodies for the intensive grass-roots canvassing and campaigning which it substitutes for money. The youth groups, and the left wing of the party generally, are handicapped by a political problem unique to this party. As it has everywhere else since the "French turn" in the thirties, the Trotskyist movement in Canada has a policy of infiltrating existing social democratic parties and "winning them to Socialism" rather than building a party of its own. They are intermittently expelled from the NDP, but since it is their policy to deny Trotskyist affiliations, and since a general air of paranoia on both sides pervades these expulsions, destructive tension and suspicion exists between the party youth and the older members, and between the legitimate left and the majority.

Conservatives. The Tories are the most interesting party in Canada, composed of an improbable number of dissident political strains. Saskatchewan, the province that elects socialists to the provincial government, votes solidly Conservative federally and is the base of a radical populist tendency in the Tories epitomized in Diefenbaker. The party has traditionally been pro-British, and contains a few old royalists who have never been reconciled to separation from Britain. It is the conservative party and contains economic right-wingers who see liberal policies as creeping socialism. It is a pro-business party and has numerous members who solicit American capital with unmaidenly eagerness.

As the pro-British party, the Conservatives have also been anti-Yankee. I don't know if it hit American papers, but Kennedy left his first official meeting with Diefenbaker in a much-reported and little-explained fury. "Informed sources" say that Kennedy politely asked Diefenbaker to stop selling wheat to China and Dief politely declined. Kennedy then not so politely insisted, and Dief said "Mr. Kennedy, you are not in Massachusetts now sir!"

The Tories didn't last long after that.

Liberals. The Liberals are roughly divided into two groups: gentlemanly civil servants and "roi-nègres" of the American empire. (There are, to all intents and purposes, no Canadian capitalists; all business-oriented politicians are of necessity servants of the Americans.) The major differences between the two groups are the degree of chagrin they feel while supporting identical policies of bowing to American political, economic and cultural control. The right wing is smooth, technocratic, competent, and bent on greasing the wheels of Manifest Destiny. The left is distressed, moral and rendered impotent by an inability to "break the rules" by informing the Canadian public of what is really going on. For instance, the liberals have opposed American intervention in Indo-China since 1952, but have spent the intervening years scampering in the wake of a succession of American presidents, whimpering and wringing their hands. In private Prime Minister Pearson refers to his conference at The Ranch as his "visit to Berchtesgaden" *(ed. note: Hitler's country retreat);* he'll do a strip-tease in the House before he says it publicly.

Communists. The Communist Party is legal in Canada, but doddering. Its death blow was the resignation of its leader in the late fifties over alleged Russian anti-semitism. Most Canadian communists are veterans of communist parties in Europe; they join ethnic political organizations but do not join the party. The young Marxists in Quebec have ignored it in favour of purely French Canadian socialist parties. Its youth movement consists almost entirely of children of party members. Sinister it isn't.

The parties and the war:

Socreds: very pro
Conservatives: anti-Communist but anti-American
Liberals: privately anti, publicly "concerned"
NDP: sincerely anti
Communists: anti

Quebec. The tendency you may have detected in this chapter to speak in terms of "Canada *and* Quebec" applies doubly to political parties. Quebec politics are Something Else. At the beginning of the Change, Quebec was right-wing nationalist. The Socreds picked up 30 seats overnight in Quebec, but lost them as rapidly. Today the political spectrum in Quebec begins where it leaves off in the rest of Canada. There is still a militant right-wing nationalist movement, but most of the nationalists and separatists have swung decidedly left, ranging all the way to terrorist would-be guerrillas. The CIA has been studying the situation.

...CULTURE...
by J.M.S. CARELESS, Professor and Chairman,
Department of History, University of Toronto

The most obvious fact about Canadian culture is that there are two, based on either the French or English language and largely kept separate by the linguistic barrier between them. Many non French-speaking Canadians (chiefly in urban areas) do have English as a second language, but the great majority of both culture groups are unilingual. French, the first language of approximately thirty per cent of the population, is chiefly centred, of course, in the province of Quebec, the basic French-Canadian homeland; though it has legal status on the federal legislature and courts, and developments now strongly under way would give it broad recognition as an alternative national language right across Canada.

There are substantial French-speaking minorities in the Atlantic provinces, in Ontario, the most populous and powerful English-speaking province, and smaller elements in the western provinces. Quebec remains the essential bastion of French-Canadian culture, although it also has its sizable, economically powerful, English-speaking minority, chiefly centred in Montreal. To complicate the cultural picture still further, immigration in the twentieth century from continental Europe has greatly added to the original French and British "founding peoples" — the Canadian phrase. While this third large ingredient has chiefly acculturated to the English-speaking majority, there is a good deal of ethnic survival among immigrant elements particularly in the prairie West, or among later comers like the concentrated Italian communities in big eastern cities, notably Toronto.

Through this immigration, there is now no one ethnic majority in Canada, the largest group, the British, having been reduced below fifty per cent of the total population. Many Americans have come as part of a two-way flow across the border that has gone on from early days; and in more recent times a sprinkling of West Indian and Asian immigrants has increased the cosmopolitan variety in Canada. All this, indeed, may make the results of the immigration process sound much the same here as in the United States. There is a good deal of similarity. The resultant cultural blend, for the English-speaking majority, looks a good deal like the Americanized product of the classic melting-pot. Yet there are differences, beginning with the fundamental English-French division, and continuing with the fuller persistence of other cultural elements in Canada. The declared Canadian ideal, at any rate, is the ethnic "mosaic", not the melting pot: the enriching power of diversity in a pluralistic society, where there is no one categorical Canadian way of life.

This may be no more than making a virtue of necessity, given the weaker absolute power of a divided and more regionalized Canadian society. Yet it at least points to the possibility of a different cultural achievement in North America. And it indicates a society that at its worst stresses ethnic difference in a narrow, even parochial way; and at its best is tolerant of difference, not expecting mass uniformity and loyalty to some unimpeachable set of national stereotypes.

Of the two major Canadian cultural communities it is worth emphasizing here that "French" and "English" are language references, not to be closely identified with French France or English England — for both communities in Canada are markedly the outgrowths of North American conditions and experience. In fact, an American entering into English-speaking Canada may come to feel that crossing the border makes little more difference culturally than going to a more remote northern state of the union. The physical surroundings, especially urban, look much the same. So do the brand names, the broad patterns of government, the social customs, the mass media spilling easily from the United States in competition with instruments like the public Canadian Broadcasting Corporation. But this brings a second point of emphasis: the same American entrant may come in for a mild form of culture shock just through assuming too much similarity. He may forget he is in another political entity, North American but not the United States. He may be irritated at Canadian uncertainty and caution, more expensive books, cars or canteloupes (the price of being Canadian). He may grow frustrated because Toronto is not New York, New Orleans, San Francisco — and fail to appreciate that while much is the same for comfort, enough is different for interest; and that a positive awareness of changes in environment is no less salutary in moving here than going to Tanzania.

Much of this English-Canadian cultural difference — limited but inherent — can be explained in terms of distinctive historical experience.

Canada not only grew with the United States, but in resistance to it from the American Revolution onward: unsure and cautious in a Canadian sense of weakness, and a fear, at first, of military conquest; willingly colonial much longer, in a need for British guarantees of power to survive and grow; always dealing with a harder landscape and a deeper internal division. This, and much more, has produced a pragmatic, less enterprising Canada, inevitably later in development than its huge neighbour.

Yet the Northern country today displays a range of intellectual and artistic activity not discreditable to a society of twenty million people divided between two cultural communities. Against the obvious charge that far fewer have achieved enormously more in other societies, one at least may note that these have been much more compact and closely knit, with less derivative, or older, traditions of their own. And while an affluent Canada with a high standard of living should be able to maintain good nation-wide cultural facilities, one should recall that affluence varies over the country, and that Canadians live chiefly in pockets of population separated by distance and natural barriers across an enormous land-mass — so that their cultural focus is more likely to be regional than national.

Whatever the limitations on Canadian culture (lessened by communications advance and public aid through agencies such as the Canada Council), English Canada has produced powerfully evocative novelists like Hugh MacLennan and Morley Callaghan: MacLennan whose novel *Two Solitudes* provided a basic name for the Canadian condition. Callaghan whose work transcends the Canadian scene. In French Canada, Gabrielle Roy's novels offer insight into a culture in rapid process of change, so different from that depicted by Ringuet before the Second World War, who epitomized and perhaps said in a final word on the older agrarian French-Canadian world. In poetry, the sweep of Ned Pratt, the urbanity of Frank Scott, the lyricism of Anne Hebert, the richness of Jean-Guy Pilon — these few names only begin a list too long to cover here.

In drama, the list would be much shorter; but younger writers and directors are making significant contributions from Charlottetown and Quebec to Toronto and Vancouver — notably, too, in films, where individual film-makers are acquiring international reputations previously only attained by some of the personnel at the National Film Board; for example, the painter-on-film, Norman McLaren. One must inevitably add the remarkably successful — perhaps now too successful — annual Stratford Festival that began with Shakespeare, in this Ontario town in the early fifties, and has since spread much wider in plays and music. Or there is the productive Royal Winnipeg Ballet and the National Ballet of Canada centred in Toronto. Montreal is particularly fertile as a centre of drama, music and the arts in French Canada; less so for English Canada, though some of the benefits of French artistic culture do spill over, especially from the magnificent Place des Arts, and from other facilities provided in Montreal during Expo — which was a considerable sign itself of growing cultural maturity in Canada.

Toronto, as a major publishing and academic centre, fulfils much of Montreal's cultural functions for English Canada and takes no second place in painting and sculpture. Its theatre, galleries, museums — and Yorkville sub-culture — give it further interest, as do its increasingly good Italian restaurants. Like most other major Canadian cities it maintains a symphony orchestra, along with opera, conservatories, and a particularly notable amount of jazz. Vancouver's cultural capabilities and limitations are somewhat comparable; but if lesser in offerings than Toronto, it has a more pleasant climate to enjoy them in.

There is not the space to go on sufficiently with quite considerable achievements in recent Canadian painting — with Borduas, Riopelle, Town and Shadbolt — or in sculpture — with Gladstone, Bieler and Vaillaincourt — or in architecture, particularly manifested in new university campuses, such as Scarborough at Toronto or Simon Fraser at Vancouver. Nor is there space to discuss the current rapid expansion of Canadian universities in size and number, nor accomplishments in scientific research, medicine and technology. One may only conclude by observing that cultural developments as various as Marshall McLuhan, the electron microscope, Banting and Best's discovery of insulin, ice hockey and the Calgary Stampede, would indicate that this is no barren wilderness to live in.

...CITIES...
by DOUGLAS MYERS, *Lecturer in Canadian History,*
Ontario Institute for Studies in Education

Canadians like to think of themselves as living close to nature, contending with the elements — a kind of North American equivalent of the Siberians or Scandinavians — with moose on Main Street, salmon or lake trout out back, and Canada geese overhead. So zealously and successfully do we foster this image that an annual ritual in the national press is the headlining of some hapless foreign visitor — usually American — who has arrived in midsummer, with the temperature in the 90's, armed — with shotguns, skis and snowshoes. In general, however, this national myth has approximately the same validity as does its American 'free enterprise' counterpart; an undeniable symbolic and psychological influence, but little connection with reality. For most Canadians are urban dwellers. The same flight from the farms and development of large congested industrial connurbations that has characterized the post-war United States has taken place in Canada, albeit at a more dignified (i.e. retarded) pace, as befits our British heritage. As a result, over 40% of Canada's 20 million people live in centres with populations of more than 100,000 and 70% live in centres with populations of 1,000 or more.

Nearly 90% of Canada's people live within 100 miles of the Canadian-American border and almost all our major cities lie strung out just beyond the U.S.A.'s northern frontier. Leaving aside Montreal and Quebec City for the moment, it is very hard to imagine what an American would find different about a Canadian city. Some visitors claim to sense a different atmosphere and pace, more relaxed and less frantic but it is very hard to identify. (*ed. note. Mr. Myers is a Canadian. Canadian cities look like what American cities look like on TV.*)

Another noticeable difference would be that, due to a negligible initial Negro population, restrictive immigration policies, and a small Indian and Eskimo population (combined it amounts to only about 225,000 people), race tension is not a major urban problem. Virtue, I hasten to add, has nothing to do with it: where sizeable racial minorities do exist (e.g. Negroes in Halifax, Nova Scotia, or Dresden, Ontario; Indians in Sault Ste. Marie or in prairie communities; Japanese on the

87

West Coast) white Canadians have reacted generally in the same manner as American whites.

Because of the natural north-south geographic division of our continent, Canadians in any region tend to have more in common economically and occupationally with Americans in areas immediately to the south than they do with Canadians in the adjoining regions. It follows then that a useful rule of thumb for an American trying to decide in which Canadian city to settle, is to think of American cities more or less directly south (e.g. Vancouver — Seattle, Toronto — Cleveland or Philadelphia; Hamilton — Buffalo, and so on). Chances are good that life in both will be pretty much the same. If one favours a New England small-city style of life then the Maritime Provinces and cities, Halifax (200,000) and Dartmouth (48,000) Nova Scotia; St John's (110,000), Newfoundland or Saint John (100,000) and Moncton (48,000), New Brunswick, are the places to choose. Average temperatures in the winter are in the low 20's and in the summer the low to mid-60's with higher precipitation (40.55 inches) than the rest of the country. Fishing, fanning, forestry and mining provide the economic base for the region, the main weakness of which is the lack of manufacturing industries. Although the provincial governments are making vigorous efforts to attract industry and are beginning to slow down their steady population loss to the U.S. and central Canada, this vulnerability was illustrated by a recent crisis over a threatened closing of a large iron and steel works at Sydney (35,000), Nova Scotia. The provincial government was forced by events to buy out the company because the closure would have thrown 3,000 men out of work, ruined Sydney, and had serious economic repercussions in the whole region.

The West Coast region of Canada stands in sharp contrast to the East, for British Columbia is one of the boom provinces with vast resources being exploited under the auspices of a flamboyant, right-wing Social Credit government. The two main cities are the capital Victoria (170,000) on Vancouver Island and the mainland city of Vancouver (840,000). The former has the reputation of being the most English city in Canada, full of retired colonels and maiden aunts, while the latter offers a combination of lotus land and gang-land qualities which make it unique in the country. Vancouver leads the country in the rates of divorce, drug addiction, alcoholism and suicide. Undeterred by this, and probably attracted by the near tropical climate (winter — low 40's; summer — low 60's) a small but active group of hippies (estimated at 1,200) and a much greater number of less spiritual hedonists have gravitated to Vancouver. With mountains behind and the ocean in front, Vancouver has a lot going for it. One internationally known English scholar and biographer at the University of British Columbia has been quoted as saying, "There aren't any intellectual demands on a writer here. There is indeed very little intellectual life among adults in Vancouver…I'm like everybody else — Vancouver's soft climate and the mountain scenery would always draw me here."

If the intensity of intellectual life tends to evaporate when faced with the delights of the West Coast, it probably is forcibly repressed when it moves east of the Rockies to Alberta. The American twins to Calgary (320,000) and Edmonton (375,000) are probably Dallas and Houston, for this is bible-punching, 'Bircher', cattle and oil country. Oil has brought many Americans — at least 75,000 — from the South-West and Calgary, with about 30,000 of them, is reputed to be the largest non-military expatriate American colony in the world. In any case, the native Albertan is more Texan than anything else. I knew one in Edinburgh who astonished the populace in general, by wearing a blue-jean suit, a Stetson, and cowboy boots, and Scottish butchers in particular, by striding to the back of their shops to cut his own T-bone steaks. All this aside, however, the foothill country is superb, the university with campi in both cities pays the highest salaries in Canada, and the Calgary Stampede is a hell of a show.

Saskatchewan is wheat country and its two cities, Regina (125,000) and Saskatoon (110,000) are tied to a wheat economy. A huge irrigation scheme and a new tar sands industry are beginning to diversify this base however. Both cities do the best with what they have, which is not much in the middle of the prairies, but a lot of tree-planting and some excellent city-planning has been done. The university is very active and lively and is expanding rapidly. The Liberal Premier who narrowly replaced the long-time farmer-socialist government in Saskatchewan, trumpets the virtues of free enterprise, is opening the province to private capital, but seems little inclined to dismantle the province's advanced social welfare framework, which includes North America's first and only socialized medical system.

Manitoba's premier city Winnipeg (300,000) achieved its prosperity as a transport and grain market centre for the west. It has a more cosmopolitan air than other Western cities due to a greater ethnic heterogenity and has retained a rather unique radical flavour (e.g.: Communists on the city council and schoolboard; a left-of-centre New Democratic Party which has an excellent chance of becoming official opposition in the next provincial election). The city has spirit sufficient to support the Manitoba Theatre Centre, the Royal Winnipeg Ballet and to host the Pan American games. The local universities are still recovering from the effects of a celebrated purge of radical academics in the 1950's, although the younger faculty are increasingly activist and outspoken. The province, as a whole, is experiencing some problems of economic stagnation but there is evidence that vigorous government action is beginning, aimed at diversifying and expanding Manitoba's economic foundation. Western winters, by the way, are harsh (average January temperature ranges from zero to 8 degrees and all the cities mentioned have recorded lows of at least 50 below zero).

The economic heartland of Canada is the fertile, rolling southwest peninsula of Ontario. With Toronto (over 2 million) and Hamilton (300,000) the largest centres, this area draws on the vast natural resources of rugged Northern Ontario, exploits the water power, transportation facilities and agricultural production of its own area, and supports about ⅓ of Canada's total population. There are more jobs, more universities, more everything here than anywhere else in the country and the climate is more moderate (winter — 20's; summer — 70's). Toronto itself is in many ways an extremely forgettable city, sprawled out on the flat north shore of the lake, with endless ticky-tacky suburbs unrelieved by scenery or imagination. In other ways, however, it is a city of many small important pleasures — quiet tree-lined neighbourhoods, clean streets, good schools, several coffee-houses and art gallery sections, excellent restaurants, several good bookstores, an island park lying off the lake-front of the city, and a magnificent city hall and civic square (built through some fit of absence of mind by an ordinarily pettifogging city council) — especially if you live reasonably centrally.

There are two universities in the immediate area, and the city's range of manufacturing, business and commercial enterprise gives the Toronto area job market great variety. One should not overlook the employment and university opportunities at smaller Ontario centres such as Ottawa (275,000 — the country's capital city — 2 universities and most government agency headquarters); London (175,000 — 1 university — insurance company headquarters); Windsor (125,000 — 1 university — automobile industry) and so on.

The most un-North American major city in Canada is Montreal (over 2½ million). The busiest inland port on the continent, it is located on a 50 square mile island by the north shore of the St. Lawrence River and contains 40% of Quebec's work force and 60% of its industry. But it is a combination of geography and culture that sets this vibrant and vital city apart. Its focus is a 'mountain' park land overlooking a brilliantly rebuilt city centre. Montreal is, in many ways, the flower of the French-Canadian political revolution and cultural renaissance which has transformed much of the life of the province in the past 7 or 8 years and which may yet carry Quebec out of the Canadian federal union altogether into separate statehood. One of the original sources of this renaissance were the radical students at Université de Montréal (there are two other universities — McGill, solid and English, and Sir George Williams) but political, literary and artistic activities now include a much wider circle and give the city a verve and panache lacking elsewhere.

Because of this dynamism, this sense of urgency and crisis, Montreal is a very exciting place to be. And yet for us (the English Canadian and the American, who are much more like each other than either is like a French-Canadian) there are certain practical problems. Montreal is the second largest French speaking city in the world (80% of its population is French speaking) and, since there seems little point in living there as part of an increasingly isolated and often stubbornly defensive English community, bilingualism is imperative. Even with a sufficient fluency, however, it is difficult to assess how acceptable one would be. The elementary and secondary school systems for example, are denominational (i.e. Catholic and 'Protestant' — all non-Catholics are 'Protestant'), though changes are being introduced which may make this more flexible. Moreover, Quebec seems to be heading into a period of economic recession. This is partly due to the let-down after the Expo-induced boom and partly due to the actions of the American, British and English-Canadian corporate and financial community which, while thunderously denouncing separatist tendencies in the provinces, are hastening their triumph by withdrawing very large amounts of investment and development capital. In a contracted job market it is conceivable that the 'outsider' might find it tough going.

...AND SNOW.

Canada is the second largest country in the world; only the Soviet Union has a greater area. Canada covers close to 4,000,000 square miles which means that it is about the same size as Europe including European Russia.

Almost half the land area of Canada is forest. Less than eight percent is occupied farm land. Much of the rest consists of rock, barren lands in the north called tundra, urban land and land used for roads. A large proportion of the world's fresh water is in Canada and the St. Lawrence River and the five Great Lakes form the most important river system in the world.

The country may be divided into six geographical regions:

Atlantic Region. The four Atlantic Provinces are almost surrounded by the sea. Except for the gently rolling lowlands of Prince Edward Island, most of the region is hilly with a rocky coastline. Some of the steep hills in Gaspe and in Newfoundland might even be called mountains. The river valleys are mostly fertile and the hills are covered with trees.

St. Lawrence Region. More than half of Canada's people live in this region of fertile fields and orchards and prosperous industrial and commercial centres. The "Niagara Fruit Belt" contains almost all varieties of fruit and many large vineyards for the production of Canadian wines. Southern Ontario is further south than all of New England, most of New York, and northern California.

Canadian Shield. The Shield takes in about half the total area of Canada and is very rocky and hilly. There is little good farm land but mineral resources abound and rivers, lakes and small streams cover the region. The northern part of the Shield lies beyond the limit of tree growth and the ground is permanently frozen except for a thin surface layer that thaws each summer.

Central Plain. The interior plains are part of a great flat area which covers the central part of the North American continent; think of Nebraska. The plains are covered to a great depth with rich black earth which provides the prairie provinces with mile upon mile of excellent farm land. It is here that much of the world's wheat is grown.

Mountain Region. The Rocky Mountains and other major ranges lie along the West Coast. Many of the peaks are over 13,000 feet high. The rocks contain rich mineral deposits and the swift mountain rivers are ideal for the development of hydro-electric power. In the valleys are some of the finest fruit growing districts in North America.

Arctic Islands. The Islands lie in the Arctic Ocean off the mainland in a great triangle. Many of them are huge. Baffin Island, for example, is almost half the size of Ontario, which is half again as large as Texas! Some of the islands have mountain ranges with peaks over 10,000 feet high.

There is nothing static or monotonous about the weather in Canada. In 1913, when 400,000 immigrants came to Canada, Kaiser Wilhelm said, "To allow these people to go to that sub-arctic country is inhuman." But temperatures have been 115 degrees in British Columbia and Alberta and temperatures often reach 100 in most inhabited places. The lowest temperature on record, reported from Snag, in the Yukon Territory, is 81 degrees below zero. The *range* is nearly 200 degrees!

Temperatures vary from one part of the country to another and even within one small area there may be an extreme change of temperature within a matter of hours. Winter is generally very cold and summer may vary from very warm to extremely hot. Fall is a distinct and pleasantly endless season. Spring is usually very short and merges quickly into summer.

Rain falls constantly on the West Coast, but the prairies suffer from summer drought. Southern Ontario and Quebec average a comfortable 35 inches annually. Except for the Pacific coast, snowfall is lightest in the Arctic (!). It is heaviest in the Maritimes and in parts of Ontario and Quebec. The snow and colder temperatures rarely occur before late November.

CITY	TEMPERATURES JANUARY MEAN	JULY MEAN	ANNUAL RAIN (INCHES)	ANNUAL SNOWFALL (INCHES)	FREEZING DATES LAST	FIRST
Prince Rupert, B.C.	36	56			Apr	Nov
Vancouver, B.C.	38	64	56	24	Apr	Nov
Victoria, B.C.	39	60	25	10	Feb	Dec
Whitehorse, Y.T.	5	56	6	44	June	Aug
Edmonton, Alta.	8	63	12	53	May	Sept
Regina, Sask.	2	67	11	40	June	Sept
Winnipeg, Man.	1	68	15	49	May	Sept
Port Arthur, Ont.	8	63			June	Sept
CHICAGO, ILL.	26	76	10	27		
NEW YORK, N.Y.	33	77	9	31		
Toronto, Ont.	25	71	25	55	May	Oct
Ottawa, Ont.	12	69			May	Sept
Montreal, Que.	15	70	32	101	Apr	Oct
Saint John, N.B.	20	62			May	Oct
Halifax, N.S.	24	65	48	64	May	Oct
Charlottetown, P.E.I.	19	67			May	Oct
St. John's, Nfld.	24	60	42	114	June	Oct
Hay River, N.W.T.	-12	61	8	35	May	Sept

THIRTY-ONE / LIVING CONDITIONS AND COSTS
IT'S A GOOD COUNTRY.
Courtesy Special Projects and Planning Branch,
Department of Economics and Development, Government of Ontario

(This chapter is really for mothers.)

STANDARD OF LIVING. In Canada life is secure. People spend a large proportion of their income and enjoy what is probably the highest standard of living in the world. Following are the percentages of households owning certain goods by country.

	CENTRAL HEATING	TELEPHONES	REFRIGERATORS
1st	Canada 75%	Canada 89%	Canada 96%
2nd	Sweden 74%	U.S.A. 83%	U.S.A. 85%
3rd	Switzerland 70%	Sweden 44%	Sweden 75%

	WASHING MACHINES	CARS	TELEVISION
1st	Canada 86%	Canada 75%	Canada 93%
2nd	U.S.A. 82%	U.S.A. 74%	U.S.A. 92%
3rd	Britain 53%	Sweden 47%	Britain 80%

The next table shows the average dollar spending pattern of a typical city family with an average income. (Incidentally, these figures can give the vigilant reader a good idea of what Canadian families are like.)

CURRENT CONSUMPTION	% OF TOTAL	CURRENT CONSUMPTION	% OF TOTAL
Food	25.6	House operation	3.8
Housing	17.5	Gifts, donations	2.7
Automobile	8.9	Recreation	2.7
Clothing	8.7	Personal Care	2.7
Personal taxes	5.7	Transportation	1.8
Furnishings	5.0	Miscellaneous	1.3
Medical Care	4.6	Reading	0.7
Security	4.5	Education	0.5
Smoking, alcohol	4.4		

WAGES. You should not come to Canada solely to earn more money, but the fact that your standard of living will be constantly increasing is significant. Between 1949 and 1965 wages increased three times faster than living costs. The average weekly wage in Ontario is $102.54 and unemployment is down to 1.8 %.

The following table shows the minimum wage rates for some common occupations in Toronto in 1966.

CONSTRUCTION TRADES (NU — Non-Union; U — Union; W — Welfare):
Carpenter — NU $2.50-3.00 hr.; U $3.58 + 5 cents W
Electrician — NU $2.75; U $4.10 + 9 cents W
Painter — NU $2.41-2.51; U $3.10 + 5 cents W

INDUSTRY AND MANUFACTURERS TRADES:

Assembler, skilled	$1.82-2.60	Mechanic (maintenance)	$2.05-2.95
Compositor	3.10-3.50	Sheetmetal Worker	1.85-2.85
Craneman	2.00-2.25	Steamfitter	2.50-3.50
Electrician (automotive)	2.00-2.50	Tool and Die maker	2.40-3.00
Machinist	1.96-2.80	Welder	1.75-2.25
Mechanic (automobile)	2.00-2.50	Technician	75.00-90.00 wk.

OTHER TRADES:
Auto Body Repairman — $1.90 – 2.50 hr.
Barber — 70% of receipts; $50.00 wk. guarantee
Cabinet Maker — $2.00-2.50 hr.
Electrical Apprentice Serviceman — $60.00-90.00 wk.
Jeweller — $2.25-2.60 hr.
Miner — $2.37 ½ hr.
T.V. Service and Repairman — $70.00-80.00 wk.

OFFICE OCCUPATIONS:

Clerk, Accounting (Male)	— intermediate	$55.00-85.00 wk.
	— senior	75.00-125.00
Typist (Female)	— intermediate	45.00-55.00
Clerk (Female)	— intermediate	55.00-60.00

The following table shows minimum monthly starting salaries for new university graduates based on offers of employment in the spring of 1966.

SPECIALIZATION	SALARY	SPECIALIZATION	SALARY
Gen. Arts and Science	$426	Engineering	$518
Agriculture	474	Library Science	470
Architecture	532	Mathematics	492
Biology	471	Medicine (M.D.)	775
Chemistry	502	Physics	510
Commerce	473	Psychology	442
Economics	469	Social Work	446
Education	442	Sociology	443

The Ontario Human Rights Code sets out laws relating to fair employment practices and fair accommodation practices. Minimum wages are set at $1.25 an hour in construction and $1.00 an hour *in all other fields*. Maximum working hours are set at eight in the day and 48 in the week. Every worker is entitled to one week's vacation with pay a year as well as a number of paid holidays. (It should be remembered that these are minimum standards only and that most workers receive wages and benefits considerably higher than the minimum.)

TAXES. The principal form of taxation is income tax. Each person is allowed a $1,000 basic deduction from his taxable income. A married man is allowed a $1,000 deduction for his wife, $300 for each child qualified to receive Family Allowance and $550 for each child not receiving Family Allowance. Below is a table showing income tax payable by some typical taxpayers in 1965.

Gross Income	Single Man	Married Man No Children	Married Man One Child	Married Man Two Children
$4000	$640	$398	$334	$271
5000	820	640	567	495
6000	1020	820	766	712
7000	1050	1020	966	903

PRICES. By comparing the following table with the table of wages you can form an estimate of what your standard of living will be.

AVERAGE RETAIL PRICES FOR CANADA — SELECTED ITEMS

Domestic gas (Toronto) average bill for the month	$13.80
Electricity (Toronto) average bill for the month	5.60
Streetcar and bus fare, one trip	.17
Taxi fare, first mile	.73
Telephone, single party line, per month	4.88
Laundry, man's shirt	.29
Dry cleaning, man's suit	1.50
Man's haircut	1.57
Woman's hairdressing —	2.68
Movie theater admission (adults)	1.25
Professional hockey admission	3.36
Newspaper, per week	.52
Cigarettes, 20	.41
Beer, dozen	2.30
Scotch, 25 oz.	6.24

ITEM	TORONTO (Dominion)	VANCOUVER (Safeway)	MONTREAL (Steinberg's)
Bread, white, sliced, 24 oz.	$.25	$.28	$.22
Butter, first grade, lb.	.69	.71	.67
Chicken, roasting, lb.	.65	.52	.49
Cookies, chocolate chip, lb.	.57	.49	.59
Corn flakes, lb.	.43	.33	.43
Eggs, dozen grade A large	.55	.48	.45
Hamburger, lb.	.59	.65	.59
Ice cream, pint	.29	.25	.27
Lamb chops, shoulder, lb.	.59	.89	.59
Milk, quart	.29	.28	.28

Oranges, dozen fresh	.69	.49	.50
Peaches, sliced, 19 oz can	.39	.32	.29
Peanut butter, creamy, lb.	.56	.45	.53
Peas, frozen petite, 12 oz. box	.30	.22	.24
Pepsi-cola, six 16-oz. bottles	.59	.67	.51
Sirloin steak, lb.	1.29	1.63	1.49
Soup, tomato, 10 oz. can	.15	.17	.14
TV dinner, beef, 11-oz. box	.75	.75	.75
TOTAL, ALL FOODS	9.60	9.58	9.03

JOBS ARE AVAILABLE...

by ROBERT D. KATZ, *employment counsellor, Department of Manpower and Immigration; and* NAOMI WALL, *Director, American Immigrants Employment Service, Toronto*

Most jobs in the U.S. have their Canadian counterparts. If you have a trade or profession it is likely that you will be able to transfer it to Canada with little difficulty. When considering your future job in Canada, it is wise to draw on your background as much as possible.

Many recent American immigrants have Bachelors Degrees. While this is certainly an asset, most immigrants to Canada have not had nearly as much education, so even with a high school diploma your opportunities remain good. If your degree is in a field such as chemistry, physics, or engineering your opportunities are excellent. For the humanities major, however, it may be more difficult, not because of lack of opportunity but rather due to lack of direction. Even with a well-defined major you will find tremendous variations in potential jobs, especially in fields such as philosophy, political science, history, or literature.

For any B.A., teaching is a possibility. All provinces have their own standards for teachers and you would do well to visit or write to the Board of Education in the province of your choice in advance. Most provinces require education courses taken within Canada before you can become a qualified teacher. This is true of Ontario, where it is necessary for you to attend the Ontario College of Education after you have acquired your B.A. It is possible to get a permit to teach in most provinces, even where further requirements are necessary, allowing you to teach on permit until you can meet the full requirements. However, these permits are granted in small communities and it is unlikely that a B.A. with no further training could teach in Toronto. It is possible to teach primary school in Quebec and the Maritimes with a B.A. or even less than a B.A. providing you have some experience with small children. The Toronto Anti-Draft Programme publishes a summary of the provincial teaching requirements.

The CAUT Bulletin includes "notices of positions vacant" and "notices of persons available for employment" and is published quarterly by the Canadian Association of University Teachers, 77 Metcalfe Street, Ottawa 4, Ontario. Subscriptions are $2 a year.

There are jobs available to high school graduates in banking, accounting, retail trade, and the food industry. There are a number of clerical positions available, which usually require some office experience. Apprenticeship and training programs are available in computing, child welfare, mechanics, banking and stock brokerage firms.

For those who have a trade, or are semi-skilled, there are a good number of jobs available. It should be noted that many trades (plumbing, mechanics, etc.) require licences and you would do well to write to the Department of Labour in several provinces and confirm that your training will be sufficient to become licenced.

When you arrive at Immigration, you will be assessed according to your intended occupation and your ability to find employment in this line of work. It would be a good idea to bring with you any letters of reference you can obtain from former employers. If you appear at Immigration with well-defined occupational goals you will be likely to receive landed immigrant status with no difficulty.

THIRTY-THREE / HOUSING
...AND SO IS HOUSING.
by ROBERT D. KATZ, *employment counsellor, Department of Manpower and Immigration, and* PEGGY MORTON, *New Left Committee*

Most Canadians do not live in caves or igloos. When you arrive you will choose among accommodations that may already seem too familiar. Still, most accommodations in Canada are cleaner than their U.S. counterparts, and — if you know where to look — less expensive.

YMCA rooms run from $3 to $4.50 a night. Weekly rates are much cheaper, usually from $15. Most large Canadian cities have several Y's. The branches are always less expensive than the central Y.

Tolerable hotel rooms run from $3 to $6 at minimum, motel rooms from $8.50. It's best to look for something permanent as soon as you can.

Single rooms without cooking facilities are cheap ($6-$11 per week) but that means eating in restaurants, which aren't good enough to justify the expense. A room with shared bath and kitchen will probably run between $9 and $15. The thing to do is share an apartment, the larger the better, or even a house. But remember with houses that heating costs will be high.

If you like older homes, try Toronto or points east. This end of Canada was built up before Manitoba became a province, and there are innumerable old flats, converted houses, basement apartments, etc. Flats, or self-contained two- and three-room apartments, will run $75 to $110 or more. A bachelor apartment in a modern building will be from $90 to $110 and a two-room apartment will probably run $105 to $130 complete. Underground heated parking in downtown apartment buildings will cost about $10-15 and outside parking $5-$7 per month.

If you like modern apartments, especially high-rises, try Toronto and points west, especially Vancouver. Vancouver residents will pay slightly more for older homes, but modern apartments will be — consistently — about $20 lower than in Toronto. And there are proportionately more of them in Vancouver.

Apartment rents vary considerably depending on the size of the community. The average monthly rental for apartments in 1966 was $109 in Toronto, $84 in London, $101 in Ottawa and $79 in Windsor.

An easy rule of thumb is that the farther east you go, the less you are likely to pay. The exceptions (as usual) are most significant about this rule. Availability in Winnipeg, Saskatoon and Edmonton is similar to Toronto and despite the increased heating costs, rent is generally 10% less.

Toronto hasn't degenerated yet, so its downtown is still a high-rent district; rents fall as you move out into the suburbs. The cheapest central area is west of Spadina or east of Yonge. West of Spadina to Christie is a fascinating area, with first-generation Italians, Portuguese, Greeks, Hungarians, etc., right next to one another. The stores and restaurants are cheaper here than elsewhere.

One problem with talking about housing costs is that they do not vary in proportion to salaries or standard of living. Toronto has the highest housing costs in Canada, but its Metropolitan Area has the highest per capita income.

71% of all dwellings are owner occupied in Ontario. But don't even consider buying a house unless you marry a millionairess. The average cost of a new home in central Toronto is $30,000, and down payments are usually substantial. Older homes are not much cheaper. The housing pinch exists everywhere in Canada to some extent, but federal subsidies may soon offset the prices.

THIRTY-FOUR / THE UNIVERSITY SCENE
THE SCHOOLS ARE PRETTY GOOD...

by JAMES LAXER, Department of History, Queen's University; past President, Canadian University Press

The chief centre for French-Canadian nationalist thought is the University of Montreal whose massive architecture dominates the northern slopes of Mount Royal. On the other side of the same mountain, McGill University, the traditional school of the privileged Quebec English, overlooks the mercantile heart of Montreal. Divided by culture and language these two universities represent the elites of the new and the old Quebec, respectively.

A thousand miles to the east, Memorial University in St. John's, Newfoundland is the first university in Canada to provide free tuition for first year students from the province. On the other side of the continent, a distance of 4,000 miles, the University of Victoria is located in the quiet, conservative setting of the capital of British Columbia. Although there are only 61 universities and colleges the vast distance that lies between the two (compared to over 1,000 in the U.S.) their diversity of curriculum, setting, size and campus life-style gives you a full range of choice.

Canadian universities have a distinguished record of making use of American resources and personnel. Dalhousie University in Halifax was founded on the tax monies collected by British officials in occupied Maine during the war of 1812. English Canada's first body of intellectuals arrived ready-made when over half the living graduates of Harvard University followed the Union Jack north in 1783.

Most Canadian universities are public institutions receiving the bulk of their funds from provincial governments; the church has left a major imprint on those institutions whose histories stretch back into the nineteenth century, but today Canadian universities are decidedly secular in tone.

Higher education in Canada is now in transition from an elite enterprise to a mass system of the kind found in the United States. Less than ten per cent of young Canadians attend universities which means that they remain largely the preserve of the relatively privileged classes.

However, the problem of numbers in post-secondary education has become a matter of concern in the past decade. The increase is being handled in part by the founding of new universities and increased enrollment at the older institutions as well as by the establishment of new programmes of post secondary education. Several provinces have set up community colleges (like U.S. junior colleges) and technological institutes.

As the number of Canadians seeking admission to universities has increased, university entrance requirements and academic standards have naturally been raised. Higher standards have also resulted from a renewed emphasis on quality education with small seminars and tutorials given by senior staff members replacing large lecture courses. This, of course, is much easier to accomplish in honours (specialized) courses at the undergraduate level, though graduate seminars are usually a reasonable size. Undergraduate and graduate education in Canada, however conservative it may appear, is in the process of being changed and there is every possibility that changes will be for the better.

In their tone, Canadian universities combine many of the features of British and American institutions as well as presenting unique home grown qualities. In terms of curriculum, classical disciplinary divisions still hold their sway and in fields such as history Canadian schools are only beginning to add non-European and non-North American courses to their rosters.

The student tends to be more the master of his time at Canadian universities than at American ones. Instead of frequent tests, essays and final exams are emphasized. In the humanities text books are less important and general reading is encouraged. The more relaxed work atmosphere vanishes suddenly about the middle of February when many students regret that the unstructured environment leaves them unprepared for finals two months later.

Graduate education is now expanding extremely rapidly. Here there are a number of differences with American schools. For one thing, the M.A. remains a degree in its own right and is not simply a stepping stone to the Ph.D. Thesis work and the research side of graduate work is emphasized and courses are not as important as in the U.S. Especially in Ontario, fellowship money for graduate students is fairly readily available after a year's residence in the province. In Canadian graduate work one university, the University of Toronto, dominates the entire field in a way that is unknown for any single institution in the United States.

Student activism has a long history in Canada. In February 1900, English and French Canadian students in Montreal armed with British and French flags fought each other in a pitched battle over disagreements about the Boer War, a war more like Vietnam for Canadians than any other, in the controversy it stirred about British imperialism.

Canadian university students have been organized at the national level for over 30 years. Today there are two national unions of students, the Canadian Union of Students (say "cuss") and the Union Generale des Etudiants du Quebec (UGEQ). Most English language universities are members of CUS, an organization that has fought for free education and other benefits for Canadian students during the last few years. UGEQ is strongly syndicalist and is strongly French-Canadian nationalist.

Student councils in Canada tend to be more powerful financially and more independent politically than in the U.S. The student council at the University of British Columbia, for example, has an annual budget of over half a million dollars, which it spends as it pleases. The student press in Canada also enjoys a long tradition of independence and it tends to be a progressive force on many campuses.

Student politics tend to less polarized in Canada than in the U.S. The student establishment has been left liberal for some years and the right wing has never had a coherent and organized voice. Though issues such as the war have been hotly debated on Canadian campuses and though draft resisters have been assisted by student councils and other student organizations, the lack of direct Canadian involvement in the war has given the issue correspondingly less impact than in the U.S.

There are a number of things to keep in mind in applying for admission to a Canadian university:

Only about half the universities will consider applications from American high school graduates. Most of the better schools insist that you complete freshman year in the U.S., or take a "western year" prep course in Canada, or transfer from another Canadian university.

The deadline for applications for admission is late, usually during the summer, and the admission requirements vary.

The academic year is divided into two terms of four months each. Some schools (Simon Fraser, Waterloo, Saskatchewan) are beginning to use the semester system.

Few university entrance awards are open to students from outside Canada. You can usually compete with Canadians for "in-course" awards after your first year, and many loan funds are available. More awards are available to American students at the graduate level.

The Canada Student Loans Act (1964) authorizes loans of up to $1000 a year to full-time university students. Loans are made to students with "satisfactory scholastic standing" who are Canadian citizens or who have resided in Canada for at least a year and intend to continue to reside in Canada. The loans are interest-free while the borrower remains a student and for six months after. The Ontario Government student loan plan (POSAP) has a similar system of loans and bursaries. Students must make a loan in order to get a bursary, but awards are often quite generous.

More information about Canadian schools can be had from the individual college "calendars" — check your library. The book *Canadian Universities and Colleges,* which summarizes the calendars of each of the schools, is available for $5 from the Association of Universities and Colleges of Canada (AUCC), 151 Slater Street, Ottawa 4, Ontario. Information on the possibilities of financial aid can be found in the following: "National Student Aid Information Service," free, from the Canadian Scholarship Trust Foundation, 300 North American Tower, 797 Don Mills Road, Don Mills, Ontario; *Study Abroad,* published by UNESCO, $4, from the Queen's Printer, Ottawa; and *Awards for Graduate Study and Research,* $3, from the AUCC.

...AND ALL OF THEM DIFFERENT.

There are 61 universities and colleges in Canada; we have listed 34 of them.

ENROLLMENT: One enrollment figure means there are no (or almost no) graduate students at the university. When there are two figures, the first represents undergraduates and the second, graduate students.

TUITION: There will probably be additional incidental fees. All figures are for undergraduate tuition for one year.

UNIVERSITY	ENROLLMENT	LIBRARY VOLUMES	TUITION
ALBERTA			
University of Alberta (Edmonton)	10,850	358,000	$300-400

One of the richest universities in Canada and strong in all academic departments, but there is a general air of stultifying conservatism. Students find Edmonton weather too cold to make hippiness possible. However, there is a small but active student left and (especially in philosophy) a few left professors, a fairly militant NDP chapter, and an active anti-war group.

University of Calgary (Calgary)	3,600	120,000	$300-400

Branch of the University of Alberta
  until 1966.

BRITISH COLUMBIA			
University of British Columbia (Vancouver)	16,350	700,000	$400-550

Not a bad school in a beautiful city. There are a number of student-power type activists on campus and the liveliest newspaper in the country. Growth is hampered by frosty relations with the provincial government.

Notre Dame University (Nelson)	630	19,200	$490

  Roman Catholic; no summer session.

Simon Fraser University (Vancouver)	2,500	70,000	$500

Handsome new university that expects 10,000 students by 1975. Students mostly left-wing; "participatory democracy" is the password and style. But...some militant teaching assistants have quit, and so has the Dean. Social sciences especially noteworthy; sociology, anthropology and political science are combined in one department with a very good staff.

UNIVERSITY	ENROLLMENT	LIBRARY VOLUMES	TUITION
University of Victoria (Victoria)	4,350	200,000	$430

Has made good progress developing its degree programmes since it ended its affiliation with UBC in 1963. Strong hippie element on campus.

MANITOBA

University of Manitoba (Winnipeg)	11,500	250,000	$374-500

Oldest but weakest of the major Prairie universities. Campus atmosphere tends to be bland and square and the setting is especially desolate in winter.

NEW BRUNSWICK

Mount Allison University (Sackville)	1,240	125,000	$540-675

United Church affiliation; in cooperation with the Maritime School of Social Work, Halifax.

University of New Brunswick (Fredericton)	6,550	150,000	$500-570

Offers doctoral programmes in English and history; present plans call for a vast improvement in facilities; the campus is one of the few in Canada to have walls and gates; students are provincial and conservative.

NEWFOUNDLAND

Memorial University of Newfoundland (St. John's)	3,950	123,000	$400

Two-year courses in agriculture and pre-forestry.

NOVA SCOTIA

Acadia University (Wolfville)	1,720	130,000	$565

Baptist affiliation; in cooperation with the Maritime School of Social Work.

Dalhousie University (Halifax)	3,720	265,000	$600

Most important university in the Atlantic provinces, with an impressive list of graduates, especially from its law faculty; medical faculty serves the whole Maritimes. An Atlantic outpost of left-wing student activists.

St.Francis Xavier University (Antigonish)	2,840	80,000	$550

Roman Catholic; well known for its pioneering work in adult education and co-operatives. .

ONTARIO

Brock University (St. Catharine's)	550	70,000	$550

Opened in 1964; a new private university, still small-townish.

UNIVERSITY	ENROLLMENT	LIBRARY VOLUMES	TUITION
Carleton University (Ottawa)	5,550	200,000	$530-590

Has developed amazingly since World War Two; distinctive programmes in public administration. School gets a good many civil servants' children. There is a strong libertarian element among students and left-wing activity tends toward organizing co-ops (most recently housing and bookstore co-ops).

University of Guelph (Guelph)	2,450	125,000	$540

Chartered in 1964; offers doctoral degrees once granted by the Ontario Agricultural College and the Ontario Veterinary College, which form the nucleus of the new university. Excellent political science department.

Lakehead University (Port Arthur)	1,350	50,000	$460

Opened in 1965; rather isolated; formerly a junior college.

McMaster University (Hamilton)	7,450	215,000	$515-600

A no-nonsense university stronger in sciences than the arts; the first Canadian university with a nuclear reactor; plans to set up a nuclear accelerator soon and open a medical school. Students tend to be solemn working-class types geared to upward mobility.

University of Ottawa (Ottawa)	11,300	340,000	$400-500

Canada's most important bilingual university, well ahead of Sudbury's embryonic Laurentian University and the College of Saint-Anne in Nova Scotia. Wide range of arts, science and professional courses; increasingly liberal atmosphere under new nonclerical charter.

Queen's University (Kingston)	6,300	500,000	$550-650

Sort of like a good Big Ten university. Famed for its achievements in both arts and science; its economics department breeds civil-service mandarins; campus atmosphere, like Kingston itself, is Whig; one of the last outposts of the Old College Spirit. Most students are football-proud and fiercely loyal. But despite the conservatism, fostered not a little by the large number of engineers (perhaps one-fourth of the undergraduate population), there have been active left groups for some years.

Rochdale College (Toronto)	1,000?	U of T Library	decided by members

Opened in 1967 as both a cooperative student residence and a radical experiment in education; each "member" responsible for deciding the direction and pace of his studies; central principle is that these decisions must be taken by the people whom they affect. Degrees not granted because the college "has no way of knowing whether prospective employers will be impressed by a member's achievement." Students range from high-school dropouts to doctoral candidates.

UNIVERSITY	ENROLLMENT	LIBRARY VOLUMES	TUITION
University of Toronto (Toronto)	16,000	1,840,000	$420-650

On par with Harvard, Berkeley, etc., by any academic standard — prestige staff, range of subject matter (Islamic studies to nuclear engineering), science facilities and strength of its graduate school. Over 350 American war exiles teach here. Canada's first multiversity with denominational arts colleges, institutes and satellites; international respect for its four-year honours-course graduates; rich, liberal, and incredibly varied — but dangerously impersonal because of its size. Independent "college" system eases this. University College, the most liberal, is the most popular among draft resisters, and its student council has given the Toronto Anti-Draft Programme $250. Many other campus groups have given money and support.

Trent University (Peterborough)	280	70,000	$550-600

Opened in 1964; mainly undergraduate, but can offer M.A. and Ph.D. "in a few disciplines." Emphasis is on close faculty-student relationships, small seminars and tutorials; there is not one lecture hall. "Our aim is to be a community of scholars," says Trent's youthful president. "This simple ideal remains relevant." Involvement is the key. Even the architecture is warm and humane. The insistence on quality at the expense of quantity (small residential colleges will remain the basic unit) and constant sense of dialogue make this one of the most attractive schools in North America — already!

University of Waterloo (Waterloo)	4,800	150,000	$555

One of the fastest-growing new universities with a good staff in most subjects and one of the best engineering schools in North America. The student council is active and left-wing and has been raising political issues for the first time. There has been a successful confrontation with the administration over bookstore prices.

Waterloo Lutheran University (Waterloo)	2,520	80,000	$520

Lutheran affiliation; degrees in arts and theology.

The University of Western Ontario (London)	11,200	500,000	$515-600

Probably Canada's most American-style university. A flourishing school of business and strong in such practical courses as journalism and secretarial science; faculty unusually divided between an entrenched reactionary set and a younger, liberal element that tends to be transient. Campus atmosphere rural and generally square except for student newspaper.

University of Windsor (Windsor)	4,620	260,000	$565-600

Undergoing rapid transformation from a Roman Catholic college to a truly non-denominational university; offers doctorates in 10 subjects, all but two in science. The students tend to be wealthy and are generally uncommitted; 12% are Americans. The fraternity type dominates the campus.

UNIVERSITY	ENROLLMENT	LIBRARY VOLUMES	TUITION

York University (Toronto) 3,500 150,000 $550
   Opened in 1960; 40,000 students expected by 1980, but staff-student ratio being held low by vigorous recruitment of specialists in Britain and the U.S. Many war exiles teach here. York is aiming (impatiently) for international distinction and demands high standards of academic performance. President Ross insists that it is still possible to make "the question of quantity a problem of quality"; his school is already pre-eminent in psychology and the natural sciences. As yet the students tend to be suburban and sober.

PRINCE EDWARD ISLAND

St. Dunstan's University (Charlottetown) 710 35,000 $400
   Roman Catholic; isolated; first-year nursing.

QUEBEC

Bishop's University (Lennoxville) 730 56,500 $450-650
   Anglican until 1947; degrees in business administration and theology.

Université Laval (Quebec City) 30,700 575,000 $350-600
   Older, smaller and more conservative than l'Université de Montréal but otherwise scarcely less illustrious in terms of academic excellence. The university is now consolidated on a modern campus and is particularly respected for its social-science departments. Despite liberal trends, the atmosphere is still clerical in emphasis, and the students are drawn from predominantly rural areas. French-speaking only.

McGill University (Montreal) 12,700 1,027,000 $400-650
   Perhaps the best-known Canadian university but beset by financial difficulties. Its arts and medical faculties are still among the best in the world. The campus is exciting and the students are the most committed and involved in Canada. The student power movement is growing quickly, mainly through an organization called Students for a Democratic University; there were recent sit-ins to support freedom of the campus press. But McGill is strongly divided on how to respond to French-Canadian demands.

Université de Montréal (Montreal) 36,400 925,000 $450-600
   Leads French-speaking universities in the number of doctorate courses offered. It has prestige staff (including top professors from Paris) and a healthy graduate school. Incubator of intellectual Quebec separatism.

Sir George Williams University (Montreal) 12,500 107,800 $450-525
   YMCA affiliation does not dominate the campus; diverse student body. Politics is growing in importance. Students recently voted to join the UGEC, Quebec's militant version of CUS, which is generally sympathetic to French demands and student syndicalism.

UNIVERSITY	ENROLLMENT	LIBRARY VOLUMES	TUITION

SASKATCHEWAN

University of Saskatchewan (Saskatoon)   20,000   313,000 $300-500

Growing fast as the province becomes richer; the campus setting, especially in the fall, is one of the country's most impressive.

Students are a mixture of farmers and left NDP types. Right-wing provincial government is threatening the autonomy of the university and keeps things interesting.

University of Saskatchewan (Regina)   3,000   100,000 $300-500

Smaller and more intimate than the Saskatoon campus, Regina is surprisingly excellent — and radical, especially in the social sciences. The school solicits in magazines like the *New York Review of Books* and has attracted a staff unique in its diversity; old and new leftists, American exiles, prairie socialists (including the provincial NDP's brain trust) as well as Defenders of the Faith. The town-gown relationship is pronounced, strained, and stimulating.

THIRTY-SIX / A HISTORY OF DRAFT RESISTANCE IN CANADA
YOU'RE NOT THE FIRST...
by ELLIOT ROSE, Associate Professor of History,
University of Toronto

In a sense it could be claimed that English-speaking Canada was founded by American political dissenters, since that is what the "United Empire Loyalists" were. As W. H. Nelson showed in *The American Tory,* the tories were a broad and diverse group, backwoodsmen and Negroes as well as aristocrats — more or less anybody, in fact, who did not fit into the farmer-patriot consensus. It would be nice to think that Canada had been deeply affected by these origins, but in fact the Loyalists figure in Canada national mythology in much the same way that the Pilgrim Fathers figure in American, and their effect on our society has been overlayed by later influences.

Between the Revolution and the Civil War, the most conspicuous "dissenters" to come North were runaway slaves. Canada had no Fugitive Slave Law, and accepted the English doctrine that a slave became free on touching free soil. It does not follow that Canadians were sympathetic to the Union cause in the war. No doubt many migrated to avoid the draft, though in that war it was rather easy to avoid. The group we know most about were Confederate partisans who came to Canada to organize raids across the border. (The U.S. claimed compensation for this at the time of the *Alabama* arbitration, but there had been raids the other way too, by Irish nationalists hoping to injure Britain.)

In the late nineteenth century, Canada like the United States received many immigrants who were known to be motivated in part by a desire to avoid conscription, in particular the heavy peacetime conscription of the Austro-Hungarian and Russian empires. Three groups stand out: the Mennonites (as common in Manitoba as in Pennsylvania), the Hutterites and the Doukhobors. The last-named came over from Tsarist Russia mainly in a single organized population-transfer. I should perhaps add that although a section of the Doukhobors has had trouble with the government and attracted a good deal of attention, the majority are law-abiding. *(Ed. note: A Canadian informant assures the editor that the Sons of Freedom, that "section of the Doukhobors (which) has had trouble with the government," is responding to a long history of injustice at the hands of the government quite comparable to that suffered by the Indians.)*

Members of these communities of military age were not automatically accorded conscientious-objector status in the two world wars, presumably on the ground that second-generation Doukhobors, or whatever, are ethnic rather than religious pacifists. Canada did resort to conscription in these wars. In a sort of a way, the draft is an old Canadian tradition, for in the early days there was (as in America) a largely ineffective law establishing a compulsory militia. But "militia" had come to mean local troops as distinct from British, and then part-time volunteers as distinct from regulars. Canada since attaining independence in 1867 has fought no war, apart from Indian wars, to protect her own direct interests and the need for a citizen-army has never been felt.

In the two world wars voluntary recruitment at first proved highly successful, especially among those numerous Canadians who identify with Britain. However, the supply of reinforcements eventually proved inadequate (this is the proper textbook way of saying "too many soldiers got killed"). Both times, allies and the military asked for Canadian conscription long before they got it; both times a political crisis resulted, chiefly because the French Canadians were unalterably opposed. The Borden government waited till 1917 (two years after Britain) to impose the draft, and although it relied very little on French votes it did not venture to face the public in a general election the same year until it had passed a special wartime voting law, giving the vote to soldiers' mothers and taking it away from German-born.

The Prime Minister in World War II, Mackenzie King, had supported Sir Wilfrid Laurier in opposition to the draft in the earlier war. At first a compromise was adopted, and those who did not volunteer for war service were conscripted for home defence. The question then became not the draft itself, but whether draftees could be sent overseas. After a long-drawnout political crisis, some were sent overseas in 1944. The total number who served outside Canada was a mere 16,000.

Since then, there has been no suggestion of reviving the draft. It was not used in the Korean war. At present the government seems disposed to reduce both regular and reserve forces rather than build them up, and the chief role they seem designed to play is as part of an international police force for the U.N. Most Canadians, I believe, are well content with this state of affairs.

THIRTY-SEVEN / CURRENT RESISTERS
...BUT YOU MAY BE UNIQUE...
by ROBERT AKAKIA, secondary school teacher,
Toronto Board of Education

In September, 1967 I began conducting a rigorous scientific investigation of what draft resisters are like. This investigation will be made fully evident with the publication of my book, *American Draft Exiles* (see Chapter 22).

The methodology of the investigation is new. It attempts to assess the philosophical and political beliefs of large groups of people and to evaluate how beliefs in certain doctrines vary with one another. I think this study will not only provide a systemic evaluation of the properties of draft exiles, but will also provide a firm empirical foundation for certain types of philosophical argument.

It is interesting to consider some of the preliminary results. I will begin with basic data. The median age of draft exiles is 21.5 years, with a spread ranging from 17 to 28 years. Their financial assets prior to obtaining a job in Canada average approximately $450. Their assets on arrival average $250.

Approximately 70% of all draft exiles have no trouble obtaining their immigration cards. 15% have some difficulty and 15% have a great deal of difficulty. It is fair to say that beginning with the use of the new unit system draft exiles have found it less difficult to obtain immigrant status.

About 37% of all exiles had been attending college when their draft boards forced them to make a decision about coming to Canada. On the other hand, 85% desire to pursue higher education in Canada. This is quite interesting as it tends to disconfirm the theory that draft exiles are college students who wanted to "drop out" of school. For it would be difficult to explain why so many of them wish to pursue further education after they come to Canada.

In a survey of their reasons for emigrating, 100% of all exiles listed their opposition to the War in Viet Nam, 85% their opposition to conscription, 67% their opposition to American Capitalism, 44% their opposition to all types of war, and 33% their fear of death. No exile emigrated because of fear of death alone.

Contrary to the popular myth, draft exiles are only significantly sympathetic to the hippie phenomenon. With respect to a control group survey of college seniors, draft exiles turn out to be relatively un-sympathetic. Few believe that there exists a hippie movement.

All draft exiles reject L.B. Johnson's position on negotiations with the North Vietnamese government (that North Viet Nam should stop fighting first). Nearly all exiles believe that the United States is the chief aggressor in Viet Nam. All draft exiles believe that the power structure in the United States determines and generates foreign policy. Most but not all exiles feel that the war in Viet Nam would continue even if President Johnson were voted out of office. On the other hand, few are willing to assign blame to anyone for the existence of the war.

The views of draft exiles concerning religion are interesting. 37% of all draft exiles are atheists; that is to say, they do not believe in the existence of any supernatural being. 26% are positivists — they do not believe that the question of the existence of supernatural beings is meaningful. And while 22% are agnostics, only 15% have any belief in any kind of god or gods. Fewer still believe in the existence of the God of the New Testament.

But these figures may be slightly misleading. It is common to suppose that all atheists are materialists, but this is not the case. First, only

40% of all draft exiles are clear about the significance of the debate between the materialists and the idealists. And of these approximately 60% are materialists and 40% are idealists. This means that only 24% of all draft exiles are materialists, considerably less than the 37% who are atheists.

Various theoretical models were constructed in an attempt to discover what types of anti-war groups are represented among the emigrants. It was found that 13% of all exiles are pacifists and 56% are radical activist types. Among the latter 40% are materialists and none are idealists.

This brief rundown indicates only a few of the conclusions which have been learned from the investigation; and indeed, some of the results stated here will have to be revised in light of new data. In *American Draft Exiles* an attempt is being made to present a definitive study of the problem, ranging over questions from ethics and logic to revolution and the theory of knowledge. It is hoped that an adequate answer to the question, "What are draft exiles like?" will be made available.

THIRTY-EIGHT / CANADIANS ON RESISTERS
...AND CANADIANS ARE INTERESTED.
by MAX ALLEN, Bookazine Enterprises, Ltd.; Abstracts Editor,
International Journal of the Addictions

When Canadians use the term "American draft dodger" it is generally free of the usual negative connotations. This is particularly noticeable in the press; even in editorials praising the moral courage of young Americans, the term "dodger" is used outright, with no attempt made to sweeten the idea or lionize the individual by calling him a draft resister or war immigrant.

It is, of course, difficult to summarize the attitude of the whole Canadian press on this issue, and it is also difficult to outline the popular consensus, as there are, as one would expect, many shades of opinion. But using the indicators available — newspaper and magazine reports and editorials, and government policy — a picture emerges of Canadians who are uncomfortable about American militarism and generally sympathetic to draft dodgers.

The issue of draft dodging is one which gets considerable attention. It makes excellent copy, and it seems to be discussed, in the press at least, more in Canada than in the United States. Some examples of stories that were carried in 1967 follow.

In November the *Star Weekly*, a national magazine of 675,000 circulation, carried a 7-page article "Five Draft Dodgers in the Flesh," together with an article "After the Draft Dodgers: American Deserters" *and* an editorial "It Takes Courage To Be a Draft Dodger."

During the summer, the Evangelism and Social Service Board of the United Church, the largest Protestant body in Canada, voted funds to aid draft resisters. Several days later, the Church's "board of directors" announced that the money would not in fact be given, since it would imply interference in the affairs of another country. A public controversy of considerable proportions ensued, during the course of which a committee of ministers of the Church was formed to deal with what it felt was unwarranted interference by the directors in the affairs of an autonomous Board. In addition, several individual congregations determined themselves to raise the money that the Church as a whole had declined to contribute.

The work of Unitarians and Quakers in various peace actions is well known, and both groups in Canada have contributed significantly to programs to aid draft dodgers.

University campuses, particularly in Toronto, are focal points for activity related to draft dodgers. Aid, in terms of contributions and expressions of support, has come from the Graduate Students Union, faculty groups, University College, and other organizations at the University of Toronto (on the other hand, in a referendum, engineering students voted 94% against giving assistance!). The president of the Students' Administrative Council, the student governing body, took the position that political issues — support for draft dodgers was the major issue — were the legitimate concern of student government. Campus discussion and argument on this point was so widespread that the president, Tom Faulkner, resigned to run again against a candidate who felt these issues were not in the province of student government. Faulkner was re-elected.

Even the RCMP seems to like young Americans. When, in October, the chairman of the Toronto Board of Education made the statement that draft dodgers were peddling marijuana in the high schools ("Draft Dodgers Selling Pot, Trustee Says" was the headline), both the RCMP and the Metropolitan Toronto morality squad made public statements to the contrary ("Police Deny Draft Dodgers Sell Drugs" was the headline the next day). Many Americans in Toronto were surprised that the police would publicly contradict a government official in this area.

Demonstrations of the kind which have become common in the United States are not yet common in Canada. The Dow Chemical recruiter was effectively picketed at the University of Toronto. And a demonstration of in excess of 5000 people marched in Toronto on October 21st in support of the march on Washington (one particularly gratifying aspect of the Toronto march was the extended applause which greeted the draft dodgers who came together as a group at the assembly point). But Canada is not actively engaged in Vietnam, so actions against that war have not reached a fever pitch. One Canadian was asked why it was so difficult to move people to act on the fact that the Canadian government was selling warplanes to America; he replied, "We've never thought our government was the moral leader of the world anyway."

Perhaps not. But the moral sense of the people and the press remains. Reflecting this was a September editorial in the *Toronto Star,* the largest newspaper in Canada: "U.S. Draft Dodgers Merit Help."

THIRTY-NINE / NEWSPAPERS AND MAGAZINES
YOU CAN FIND OUT MORE . . .

Calgary Herald, 7th Avenue and 1st Street S.W., Calgary, Alberta. $20.80 a year.

Canadian Dimension, P.O. Box 1413, Winnipeg, Manitoba. $3.15 a year. *Journal of the intellectual left-wing of the Canadian social democratic party (NDP).*

Charlottetown Guardian, Charlottetown, Prince Edward Island. $20.80 a year.

Edmonton Journal, 10006 — 101st Street, Edmonton, Alberta. $20.80 a year.

Halifax Chronicle-Herald, Halifax, Nova Scotia. $20.80 a year.

Maclean's Magazine, 481 University Avenue, Toronto 2, Ontario. $3.00 a year. *Popular news and opinion monthly, well-respected, which has no American equivalent.*

Montreal Gazette, 1000 St. Antoine Street, Montreal, Quebec. $23.40 a year.

Montreal: Le Devoir, 434 Notre-Dame East, Montreal, Quebec. $3.00 a month. *Leading French language daily; doesn't depend on American news services.*

New Left Committee Bulletin, 658 Spadina Avenue, Toronto 5, Ontario. $3.00 a year (monthly). *Canadian version of New Left Notes. The New Left Committee is SUPA's successor.*

Ottawa Citizen, 136 Sparks Street, Ottawa 4, Ontario. $3.00 a year.

Our Generation (Against Nuclear War), 3510 rue Ste-Famille, Montreal 18, Quebec. $5.00 a year (quarterly). *Pacifist-oriented journal.*

Regina Leader-Post, 1964 Park Street, Regina, Saskatchewan. $20.80 a year.

Saint John Evening Times-Globe, Saint John, New Brunswick. $26.00 a year.

Saint John's Evening Telegram, 277 Duckworth Street, St. John's, Newfoundland. $12.50 for six months.

Saturday Night, 55 York Street, Toronto 1, Ontario. $2.50 a year (monthly). *Canadian version of the Saturday Review.*

Star Weekly, 80 King Street West, Toronto 1, Ontario. $10.40 a year (weekly). *Canadian version of the New York Times Magazine.*

This Magazine Is About Schools, P.O. Box 876, Terminal A, Toronto 1, Ontario. $3.50 a year (quarterly). *Friedenberg: "The best, freshest and most penetrating journal dealing with education that I have seen in years."*

Toronto Daily Star, 80 King Street West, Toronto 1, Ontario. $3.00 a month. *Small-l liberal paper on a large-L Liberal leash.*

Toronto Globe and Mail, 140 King Street West, Toronto 1, Ontario. $3.00 a month. *Probably the best English-language newspaper in North America.*

Toronto Telegram, 440 Front Street West, Toronto 1, Ontario. $3.00 a month. *Instructive contrasts with flag-waving U.S. equivalents.* ·

Vancouver Sun, 2250 Granville, Vancouver, British Columbia. $3.50 a month.

Victoria Daily Times, 2631 Douglas Street, Victoria, British Columbia. $27.00 a year.

Winnipeg Tribune, Smith and Graham Streets, Winnipeg, Manitoba. $10.50 for 3 months.

FORTY / FOR FURTHER READING
...IN BOOKS.
—from w. d. GODFREY, *Assistant Professor of English Literature, University of Toronto**

Six books to describe a country:
  Morley Callaghan, *Morley Callaghan's Stories* (Macmillan)
  Mordecai Richler, *The Apprenticeship of Duddy Kravitz* (McClelland and Stewart)
  Margaret Laurence, *The Stone Angel* (McClelland and Stewart)
  Leonard Cohen, *Beautiful Losers* (McClelland and Stewart)
  Hector de Saint-Denys-Garneau, *The Journal*
  Dennis Lee, *Kingdom of Absence* (Anansi Press)

Callaghan's stories are set in the Toronto of the twenties and thirties, but are the deepest probing yet achieved by a Canadian author of what makes the average human being dream and function; Richler's novel is a comic, 'growing-up' novel set in Montreal's Jewish and Goyish communities, showing very effectively how one grinds against the other;

* Dave Godfrey was co-founder of House of Anansi Press.

The Stone Angel is one of a number of good Canadian novels describing prairie life and the effects of isolation and ambition upon the individual; Cohen's poetry is reflected in this novel, which is probably too well-known to need description; *The Journal* is only one of many exciting ways for the non-French speaking reader to begin to explore the vast body of French-Canadian literature; *Kingdom of Absence* is a very recent collection of poetry which shows, among many other revelations, just what the problems are for someone existing, thinking and feeling in modern Canada.

—from PEGGY MORTON, *New Left Committee*

Dominion of the North: A History of Canada, by Donald Creighton (Toronto: Macmillan & Co., 1962). One of the best general histories of Canada.

The Canadian Identity, by W.L. Morton (Toronto: University of Toronto Press, 1961). Nationalist's interpretation of Canadian history.

Lament for a Nation, by George Grant (Toronto: McClelland and Stewart, 1965). Conservative's eloquent argument for Canadian independence.

Peacemaker or Powdermonkey, by James Minifee (Toronto: McClelland and Stewart, 1960). Interesting study of Canadian foreign policy, especially vis-à-vis the U.S.

The Smug Minority, by Pierre Berton (Toronto: McClelland and Stewart, 1968). Best-selling liberal critique of Canadian society.

The Vertical Mosaic, by John Porter (Toronto: University of Toronto Press, 1965). Excellent study of class and power in Canada.

APPENDIX

A. EXCERPTS FROM THE CANADIAN EXTRADITION TREATY

The extradition treaty between Canada and the U.S. and its six amendments can be found in the appendix of G. V. Laforest, *Extradition To and From Canada*, 1961, Hauser Press, New Orleans, or in a law library, scattered in *U.S. Statutes* and *U.S. Treaties.*

A person in Canada can be extradited to the United States if he is accused or has been convicted of a crime which is listed in the treaty and which was committed within the jurisdiction of the United States.

The treaty lists the following crimes.

1. murder, or assault with intent to commit murder

2. piracy

3. arson

4. robbery

5. forgery, or the utterance of forged paper

6. manslaughter when voluntary

7. counterfeiting or altering money; uttering or bringing into circulation counterfeit or altered money

8. embezzlement; larceny; receiving any money, valuable security, or other property knowing the same to have been embezzled, stolen, or fraudulently obtained

9. fraud by a bailee, banker, agent, factor, trustee, or director, or member or officer of any company, made criminal by the laws of both countries

10. perjury, or subornation of perjury

11. rape, abduction, child stealing, kidnapping

12. burglary, housebreaking, or shopbreaking

13. piracy by the law of nations

14. revolt, or conspiracy to revolt, by two or more persons on board a ship on the high seas, against the authority of the master; wrongfully sinking or destroying a vessel at sea, or attempting to do so; assaults on board a ship on the high seas with intent to do grievous bodily harm

15. crimes and offenses against the laws of both countries for the suppression of slavery and slave-trading

16. (a) obtaining property, money or valuable securities by false-pretenses or by defrauding the public or any person by deceit or falsehood or any fraudulent means would or would not amount to a false pretense; (b) making use of the mails in connection with schemes devised or intended to deceive or defraud the public or for the purpose of obtaining money under false pretenses

17. wilful and unlawful destruction or obstruction of railroads which endangers human life

18. procuring abortion

19. bribery, defined to be the offering, giving, or receiving of bribes made criminal by the laws of both countries

20. offences, if made criminal by both countries, against bankruptcy law

21. wilful destruction or wilful non-support of minor or dependent children

22. crimes and offenses against the laws for the suppression of the traffic in narcotics

The treaty states that:
"Extradition is also to take place for participation in any of the

crimes mentioned... provided such participation be punishable by the laws of both countries."

"No person surrendered... shall be triable or be tried for any crime or offence committed prior to his extradition, other than the offense for which he was surrendered."

B. OCCUPATIONS IN STRONG NATIONAL DEMAND

The cancellation of graduate deferments has helped the chances of young, unskilled immigrants. The university graduates, who are already qualified to enter Canada, will go to the top of the draft rosters, and the less-qualified prospective immigrant has now been given time to acquire training or experience in a trade needed in Canada.

Many of the occupations on this list require a degree or extended training, but some of them can be acquired in six months to a year. Letters of reference or formal training certificates in any of these high demand fields should guarantee entry of an applicant. In obtaining such letters from former employers, the applicant should be careful that the *specific* skills he practiced are cited in the terms used in this list. Applicants with farming experience should have it specified that they are familiar with the specialized equipment used on a modern, mechanized farm.

The occupations in high demand are subject to constant fluctuations. For instance, draughting and welding have been deleted, but may return to the lists within the next few months if the construction industry rallies. A skilled worker whose occupation is not on this list should not be too worried. The point system allows up to 10 points for skills independent of current demand, in recognition of the continuing value of the investment of time and money to acquire such a skill.

Professional, Technical, and Related Workers

Electronic engineer	Mining engineer
Telecommunication engineer	Engineer, petroleum and natural gas
Mechanical engineer	Chemist
Chemical engineer	Geophysicist
Metallurgist	Biologist, general
Ceramic and glass engineer	Bacteriologist

Silviculturist (forester)
Landscape planner
Physician, general practice
Surgeon, general
Medical or surgical specialist
Physiologist, medical
Pathologist, medical
Toxicologist
Dentist
Professional nurse
Practical nurse
Nurses, non-professional (psychiatric)
Physiotherapist
Occupational therapist
Dietician
University teachers
Teacher (nursery school)
Teacher (primary school)
Teacher (secondary school)
Teacher (trade school)
Teacher of (mentally and physically handicapped)
Technician (industrial radiographer or other non-destructive tester)
Technician (research laboratory)
Technician (medical laboratory technologist)
Technician (industrial laboratory)
Social worker
Librarian
Economist
Statistician
Sociologist
Mathematician
Psychologist
Personnel specialist, industrial
Occupational analyst
Translator
Designer (industrial and commercial products)
Quantity surveyor
Computer programmer

Clerical Workers
Stenographer-typist
Secretary, stenographic
Typist

Sales Workers
Salesman (insurance)
Salesman

Farmers, Fishermen, Hunters, Loggers and Related Workers
Master gardener
Landscape gardener
Farm-hand, general
*Farm-hand (vegetable), or market garden
*Farm-hand (fruit)
Farm-hand (livestock, general)
Farm-hand (dairy farm)
Farm-hand (poultry)
Nursery worker
Gardener
*For a few weeks in the Spring and early Fall, the demand for these occupations is extremely high.

Miners, Quarrymen and Related Workers
Miner, general (hard rock)

Workers in Transport and Communication
Pilot (aircraft)
Radio broadcasting station operator
Television broadcasting station operator

Craftsmen, Production Process Workers and Labourers — Not Elsewhere Classified
Loom fixer
Knitter, power-driven machine
Dyer
Tailor
Cutter (fur)
Upholsterer (furniture)
Upholsterer (vehicle)
Patternmaker (garments)
Marker (garments)
Cutter, ready-to-wear garments (except leather)
Cutter, gloves
Sewing-machine operator

Moulder, metal foundry
Coremaker, hand, metal foundry
Coremaker, machine, metal foundry
Maker and repairman, precision
　instruments
Maker and repairman, optical
Maker and repairman, orthopaedic
　appliances
Maker and repairman, dental pros-
　thesis (dental technician)
Fitter-assembler, precision
　instruments
Serviceman, precision instruments
Fitter-machinist
Toolmaker
Die maker
Patternmaker (metal) foundry
Maker (metal) machine shop
Metal working — setter-operator, any
　machine tool
Fitter-assembler, metal products
Erector and installer, machinery
　(millwright)
Mechanic-repairman, metal products,
　general
Mechanic-repairman, metal (working
　machine tools)
Mechanic-repairman (aircraft
　engines) aircraft maintenance
　engineer)
Mechanic-repairman (internal com-
　bustion engines)
Mechanic-repairman (turbines)
Mechanic-repairman (motor vehicles)
　(gasoline)
Mechanic-repairman (motor vehicles)
　(diesel)
Mechanic-repairman (heavy duty
　equipment)
Sheet-metal worker, general
Sheet-metal worker (aircraft)
Sheet-metal worker (vehicle) (auto
　body repairman)
Pipe fitter
Welder, gas and electric
Structural-steel worker, workshop

Shipwright, metal
Ship plater
Plate bender, steel
Tool grinder, machine tools
Electrical repairman
Electrical fitter
Electronics fitter
Electronics fitter (radio and television
　transmitters and radar equipment)
Electronics fitter (industrial
　equipment)
Mechanic-repairman, radio and
　television
Shipwright, wood
Boatbuilder, wood
Carpenter, bench
Cabinetmaker
Woodworking-machine, setter-
　operator, general
Lathe setter-operator, woodworking
Spindle-carving machine setter-
　operator, woodworking
Woodworking-machine operator,
　general
Patternmaker, wood
Furniture finisher, wood
Baker
Butcher
Paper makers
Laminator (plastics)
Extruding-machine operator (plastics)
Moulding-machine operator (plastics)
Stationary-engine operator (internal
　combustion or reciprocating steam)

**Service, Sport, and Recreation
　Workers**
Head cook
Cook (except private service)
Cook (private service)
Household Assistant (except private
　service)
Household Assistant (private service)
Household Assistant (personal)
Nursemaid
Beautician

IF YOU'RE A YOUNG AMERICAN WHO'D LIKE TO LIVE ON A COMMUNAL FARM, make sure to get in touch with Isabel Alonzo, 28 Woodlawn Avenue, Toronto 7, Ontario (416) 921-6732. Mrs. Alonzo's husband was instrumental in setting up the still-successful commune at Argenta, British Columbia. Now she has plans for a 200-acre abandoned farm in the rolling hills and forests of Georgian Bay, 95 miles north of Toronto. Hopefully the farm will open this spring or summer. "It will have to be done very gradually," Mrs. Alonzo writes. "Most new settlers will have to support themselves first by getting jobs in nearby towns and farming in their free time.

"One boy I spoke to on the phone makes me realize that some youngsters have a very romantic notion of what settling on the land entails, and a few practical words of guidance as to how to prepare themselves might not be amiss. The permanent settlers will have to be selected among those with a sincere love of country living, who are prepared to work hard, and to collaborate with others, and who really enjoy using tools and are prepared to acquire some skills...."

AFTERWORD
BRINGING DRAFT DODGERS TO CANADA IN THE 1960S: THE REALITY BEHIND THE ROMANCE

BY MARK SATIN

Several lifetimes ago, my "job," calling, and passion was bringing American draft dodgers to Canada.

In April 1967, as a 20-year-old American Vietnam War resister in Toronto, I was named head of the Student Union for Peace Action's Anti-Draft Programme; and after SUPA disbanded that September I co-founded and became first director of the Toronto Anti-Draft Programme (TADP).

SUPA was Canada's premier New Left political organization in the 1960s, with interests ranging from community organizing to foreign policy. Its Anti-Draft Programme had been established in 1965 to handle inquiries from young Americans interested in immigrating to Canada as an alternative to serving in the U.S. military.

At first the Programme lagged behind independent anti-draft groups in Vancouver and Montreal — for example, Vancouver produced the best how-to-immigrate brochure, and Montreal established the first draft-dodger hostel. However, under my direction the Programme's capacities and visibility rapidly expanded. By late 1967 the reconstituted

TADP had become Canada's (not to mention the world's) largest pre-immigration counseling and post-immigration assistance organization for U.S. draft resisters and military deserters.

Long, quasi-sympathetic articles in newspapers like the *Toronto Star*, the *Los Angeles Times*, and *The New York Times* made our efforts sound positively heroic.

This article is about the reality behind the romance. It is about TADP's efforts (heroic and otherwise), but it is also about what happens when there's a lack of empathic personal, cultural, and political connection within even the most "idealistic" social change organizations. It is about the stubborn realities of human nature. It is about Life.

A. THE GATHERING STORM

When the Programme's board hired me in the spring of 1967 (it had been making do with a very part time letter-answerer since late 1966), they didn't really know what they were getting. I looked and sounded like a dedicated 20-year-old activist, and I certainly was that, civil rights volunteer for the Student Non-violent Coordinating Committee (SNCC) in Mississippi, president of a chapter of Students for a Democratic Society (SDS), etc.

But I was also a natural-born American social entrepreneur, in love with the likes of Ben Franklin, Tom Paine, and William Lloyd Garrison, and within a few months I'd turned the Programme from a rather pokey entity averaging fewer than three inquirers per day, into one of the most visible, energetic, and effective organizations in the anti-war movement, averaging well over 50 phone calls, letters, and visitors per day through the last 10 months of my time there.

I also conceived and wrote the *Manual for Draft-Age Immigrants to Canada* (published jointly by TADP and the House of Anansi Press in January 1968) and helped turn it into a huge bestseller; both the Toronto *Globe and Mail* and the *Toronto Star* have reported that nearly 100,000 copies were distributed overall.

Alas, as in many social change groups of that era, things were not as rosy as they seemed.

The Programme's board consisted largely of socialists and pacifists. I considered myself post-socialist and situational-pacifist.

The board felt deeply conflicted (to put it mildly) whenever heroes of theirs such as Tom Hayden of SDS, Stokely Carmichael of SNCC, and folksinger Joan Baez urged draft resisters to go to jail or go "underground" in the U.S., rather than immigrate to Canada. Two board members actually opposed printing the *Manual* because of SDS's opposition to Canadian immigration; one of them characterized SDS as our "vanguard" organization whose positions we were duty-bound to follow. I deeply felt and vociferously argued that a mass movement of young Americans to Canada could help end the war — and anyway, I couldn't have cared less what the political left wanted me and the resisters I nurtured to do with our lives.

Finally, and perhaps most crucially, the Canadians on the board mistrusted what they called "rabble-rousing," and feared it could get the border shut down. I believed that in order to reach ordinary young Americans (i.e., the kinds of kids I grew up with in Moorhead, MN, and Wichita Falls, TX), we had an *obligation* to make ourselves as visible as possible.

In addition, I thought the board's concern about the border was a vestige of far-left paranoia. Most war resisters were middle class, reasonably well educated, moderately ambitious, preternaturally sincere, and eminently employable, and Canadians welcomed us wholeheartedly, a beautiful thing. They even seemed to enjoy tweaking the Americans over the draft dodger issue (even as they continued shipping war supplies to the U.S.).

Thus the stage was set for an ongoing battle, behind the scenes, between the board and me; and it never let up. Here is an alphabet soup of the things I said or did that managed to baffle, offend, outrage, or alienate board members:

B. POINTS OF CONTENTION

1. JOB DEFINITION

    a.   My insistence that we provide help to military deserters and not just draft resisters (the board feared this could get us in trouble with the Canadian government);

    b.   My insistence on turning the office into a warm and welcoming environment, with couches, sleeping bags, a wall-size Canadian flag, a floor-to-ceiling peace symbol made of exiles' draft cards, and a hotplate (the board did not want me to encourage people to "hang out." One board member was especially incensed about the hotplate. "It feels like a soup kitchen!" he shouted at a board meeting, his arms waving wildly. I had to work hard to stifle my laughter);

c. My insistence on devoting as many resources to post-immigration assistance as to pre-immigration counseling (before I changed the culture, that was not their m.o. One board member, a former SUPA anti-draft counselor, liked to say we shouldn't be "baby sitters" for draft resisters. Another board member explained her attitude this way: "Americans are like little children. You can't always be holding their hands");

d. My plea that the board hire a professional bookkeeper (all I knew how to do in those days was keep a primitive list of income and outgo. The board agreed to "try" to obtain one but never managed to do so during my tenure there. It was much more energized by my unauthorized "takeover" of unused space in the SUPA building beginning the week two television crews were scheduled to interview me. One board member and SUPA employee called me a "little imperialist," to the general delight of the board);

e. My proposal that we encourage the formation of a visible and vibrant neighborhood of "American exiles" in Toronto, the better to telegraph our existence and our message to the folks back home and to the international community (this proposal, which I made the week before I was hired, almost killed my chances of employment. As one board member put it, "We want draft resisters to just fade into the Canadian woodwork!" A couple of years later, a so-called "American exile ghetto" did emerge around Beverley Street near the University of Toronto);

f. My unabashed encouragement of the formation of a political organization for war resisters (it too sprang up in due course, as the Union of American Exiles, "Amex" for short);

g. My working the same number of hours each week that young top-tier journalists and lawyers did, and do (polar opposite of "movement hours" — especially in the 1960s!);

h. My allowing some of the most problematic war resisters to sleep in the office, such as an underage girl, a guy who'd driven up in an ice cream truck filled with dead rabbits floating in formaldehyde, and a poorly trained dog named Watts;

i. My writing at least a couple of personalized sentences to nearly everyone that wrote us, even when our literature and form letters appeared to answer every question they might have;

j. My sending form letters to 500 U.S. radio stations asking to be on their talk shows (a great way to reach ordinary Americans, I argued; but board members saw it as shameless self-promotion. They also worried that it might tempt The Authorities to Crack Down. Wasn't the underground press enough?);

k. My sending what was, in effect, a five-page direct-mail fundraising letter, something I'd never seen or even heard of before, to a random sample of 50 people on our 400-person mailing list (no matter that it raised $2,000, over $14,000 in today's dollars — "I've never seen anything like this before!" one board member roared at me after charging into our office, which was full of guys waiting to be counseled. "Who cares about your background? Or what goes through the minds of these kids at night? . . . Who do you think you are?" It would be another decade before the North American left began making use of emotionally resonant direct-mail);

3. MANUAL

l. My going ahead and writing the *Manual* even after I'd been told, at a board meeting, that our flimsy and woefully inadequate little brochure was quite enough and that a more substantial publication could get the border shut down, and us shut down;

m. My inviting board members to come to the office and review the final draft of the manuscript (their response was eloquent: not one of them showed up);

n. My sending unsolicited review copies of the *Manual* to hundreds of journalists and 2,000 draft counselors across North America (supposedly another Mark Satin ego trip);

o. My imploring the board to print 30,000 copies of the second edition, given that *12,000 copies were already on back order* and that a major Canadian printer who'd heard me speak at a church had promised to do one, and only one, print run for me, on supermodern machinery, at a bargain-basement price (in the end I was lucky to get the board to agree to a print run of 20,000. If you're wondering why the once-ubiquitous second edition looks less like a movement publication than a government one, with semi-gloss paper and an exquisite typeface, well . . .);

4. MEDIA

p. My incessant use of the mainstream Toronto and U.S. media to publicize our existence and our work — for examples, see page one of *The Globe and Mail* for October 11, 1967, and page seven of *The New York Times* for February 11, 1968);

q. My comfort level with mainstream reporters (in those days, the far left was extremely wary of the press. A SUPA staff member once told me, "Mark, the *Globe and Mail* and the CBC are the *enemy!*");

r. My willingness to say what I thought and felt to those reporters, rather than regurgitate talking points to them;

s. My conviction that, in the U.S. media, even negative publicity was good publicity, since it let guys know where to go for help;

t. My eagerness to take public issue with pacifist and left-wing opposition to draft resisters immigrating to Canada;

u. My attempt, in an interview in a *New York Times Magazine* article, to put some distance between the Anti-Draft Programme and the far-left forces within SUPA;

v.   My leading a long procession of war resisters to a "love-in"
     on the University of Toronto campus, then conducting a mar-
     riage ceremony there for a hippie-looking war-resister couple
     (you can see the once "controversial" *Globe and Mail* photo of
     their embrace opposite page 201 in Canadian historian Pierre
     Berton's book *1967: The Last Good Year*, published in 1997);

w.   My reimbursing myself, after the *Manual* had generated thou-
     sands of dollars, for $324 that I'd personally spent on office
     supplies and on unreturned loans to destitute war resisters — all
     documented — over a nine-month period;

x.   My moving in with one of Toronto's most visible radical fem-
     inists, a 27-year-old former SUPA staffer and critic of the
     organization named Heather Dean (for more on Heather, see
     Gary Dunford, "Heather Dean Doesn't Like the Way YOU Live,"
     Toronto Star, July 1, 1967, special "Second Century" section, p. 71);

y.   My entering the premises of one of SUPA's successor organiza-
     tions, the New Left Committee, through a window at 9:15 in the
     morning to use a mimeograph machine that I was authorized to
     use (and inadvertently breaking the window... not very smart);

z.   My attempt to reconstitute the board, after SUPA collapsed,
     so it would include fewer political radicals and more repre-
     sentatives of mainstream Canadian society — specifically, a
     co-founder of House of Anansi Press (publisher of the *Manual*
     and of Margaret Atwood); a Toronto entrepreneur; an ally at
     the Canadian Department of Manpower and Immigration; a
     renowned Canadian historian; and an attorney rather than a law
     student. All five had contributed guest pieces to the second edi-
     tion of the *Manual* (the board threatened to sue my counseling
     partner and me if we carried out our plan. They meant it, too.
     They'd have probably lost, but they'd have pulled the Programme
     down with them; so we had no choice but to give in).

C. IN PERSPECTIVE

By now I'm sure you get the picture. It was a culture clash. Within weeks, I had become a personification for the board of Amerikan arrogance and overreach and irresponsibility; and they had become, for me, a personification of Canadian timidity, under-reach, stodginess, fearfulness-coupled-with-resentment, and refusal to dream big dreams.

It was also a generational clash — I was the only true Baby Boomer among them. It was the supercilious fathers and mothers against the rebellious son. Except in this case, the fathers and mothers were the ones with the hyper-left-wing politics. (Our most "conservative" board member once began a board meeting by reading, only half-humorously, from a devotional — the *Little Red Book* of Chairman Mao.)

Every night when I'd walk home (and it was often close to midnight), draft dodgers' confidences and words of appreciation would be ringing in my ears — and I'd feel the Sword of Damocles hanging over my head because of the smoldering disapproval and resentment of most of the board members.

I knew my place at the Programme couldn't, and wouldn't, last much longer, and my "solution" was to devote myself ever more completely to caring for the exiles, sometimes even bringing them home with me (which Heather rarely appreciated!). I was indifferent to many board members' romantic heroes — Fidel Castro, Mao Zedong, Louis Riel — but I did absolutely feel like one of my own boyhood heroes, Holden Caulfield (of J. D. Salinger's novel *Catcher in the Rye*), standing on the edge of a rye field and catching all the young people before they fell off the cliff and did irreparable damage to their lives . . . and to Vietnamese lives.

The end, when it finally came in May 1968, was uglier than I'd imagined. (Remember, I was only 21 and a product of kindly small towns in the American Midwest.) I was fired at a board meeting for ridiculously trumped-up reasons — the only one they really meant was "arrogance" (their word). The two board members who voted to keep me were the only ones who'd actually worked with me, my counseling partner and the head of our job-finding service.

One member of the board, a married Trotskyite who'd spent years trying to bed the woman I'd moved in with, vowed to erase me from the organization's memory (several board members nodding their heads in stern approval), and within a few weeks thousands of letters that I'd answered or caused to be answered, many with my notes jotted on them, "mysteriously" disappeared from our office, never to resurface.

A rumor was started that I'd quit TADP because of "burnout." In addition, my name was removed from the title page of most future editions of the *Manual*, and a rumor was started that I was only the nominal author or that I'd based it on SUPA's earlier work. Those tall tales diminish academic books and articles to this day.

Although I'd left all my drafts of the *Manual* behind in carefully-marked manila file folders, along with my ruthless edits of the guest chapters I'd solicited and comments on the manuscript from nine draft counselors across North America, "somehow" none of that material made it into TADP's historical file at the University of Toronto library, the Jack Pocock Memorial Collection, named after a radical Quaker activist who was the second person on our board who vowed to fire me. That was in September 1967 — just after I'd appeared on the cover of a glossy Canadian magazine. His wife, the keeper of the file, was the first, in May 1967 — three days after I'd been pictured and profiled in a long article in *The New York Times Magazine*.

Given all that, I was, and remain, remarkably unbitter. We did help stop the war, and that was the main thing. In the fall I moved to Vancouver and started "The Last Resort," a 50-bed-and-pallet hostel for draft dodgers and military deserters. By the early 1970s I'd begun work on a book called *New Age Politics: Healing Self and Society*. It was eventually published in Canada, the U.S., Sweden, and Germany.

I know, now, that I was partly at fault for what happened between the board and me. In those first years of my adult life I lacked the personal and social skills to communicate well with the kinds of people that were on the board — not to mention the patience; though it might have helped if even one of them had tried to honestly communicate with me.

It must have been difficult for them to watch me, a small, woefully undereducated Amerikan kid with unkempt hair and torn clothes, get myself and the Programme into the *Toronto Star* at least 10 times, while the causes they deeply cared about often failed to get the coverage they deserved. (The Programme fell completely off the *Star*'s radar screen after I was fired.)

It hurt me, more than I knew at the time, that not one board member ever thanked me for writing the *Manual* — even after it was clear that the *Manual* would be helping to support their efforts for years to come.

I did appreciate, and continue to appreciate, the lesson in human nature that the board inadvertently taught me — that no matter how "noble" our politics, we are all still and shall forever remain the deeply flawed creatures of the Old Testament. In fact, for reasons only novelists can fully explain — Dostoevsky, Silone, Orwell, Solzhenitsyn, others — the Seven Deadly Sins may be most prevalent among those whose politics are most "noble." (Or try my Jungian friend Connie Zweig's anthology *Meeting the Shadow*.)

There were other lessons too, but I leave it to you to figure them out. If you are a young idealist, you will need them for your journey.

ACKNOWLEDGEMENTS

The Toronto Anti-Draft Programme wishes to thank the following for their comments on and additions to Part One: Robert Bird, CO Services, American Friends Service Committee, Philadelphia; Steve Gompertz, Draft Counsellor, S.D.S. Anti-Draft Union, Berkeley; C.J. Hinke, Administrative Director, Resist / Support-in-Action, New York City; Joe Kearns, Youth Secretary, War Resisters League, New York City; Frank Nussbaum, Draft Counsellor, Boston Draft Resistance Group; John Reints, CO Counsellor, Central Committee for Conscientious Objectors, Philadelphia; Joe Tuchinsky, CO Counsellor, American Friends Service Committee, Chicago.

The Programme wishes to thank the professors and other Canadians who contributed original chapters to Part Two; their names have been cited with their texts. Kenneth McNaught, Professor of History and an editor of *Saturday Night Magazine*, made a number of valuable additions and Mr. Paul Chisholm of the Ontario Department of Economics and Development steeped us with relevant literature. Eric Marks in Toronto and Mrs. Ed Miller of the Montreal Council to Aid War Resisters did some of the research.

Special credit must go to the Vancouver Committee to Aid American War Objectors, whose corrections and additions were invaluable.

Additions, 2017: It is unconscionable that, even in the pre-feminist 1960s, I failed to acknowledge my Canadian partner-lover-confidante, Heather Dean, for putting up with me and my $25-a-week salary while I tried to save the world by counseling draft dodgers 12/7 and writing this book. Thanks also should have gone to some of the amazingly caring war resisters whose volunteer work at the Anti-Draft Programme office made my writing time possible. I'm thinking of you Larry Aulten, Bob Eyer, Bernie Jaffe, John Poteau, Mike Rosenbaum, Gene Thomas, John Tiller, Dick Todd, Les Whittington, and Tom Zimmerman. Hope most of you are still with us.

Another unconscionable oversight is that I failed to acknowledge Dave Godfrey, co-founder of Anansi Press, for daring to help produce this book. Without Anansi's imprimatur, the *Manual* could never have become a mainstream-media phenomenon or been perceived as sufficiently trustworthy by young Americans. For the 2017 edition, I rush to thank Anansi's Sarah MacLachlan, Amelia Spedaliere, Matt Williams, and Maria Golikova. While Dave had to deal with a headstrong 20-year-old, that was probably easier than having to deal with a cantankerous 70-year-old.

MARK SATIN is an American political theorist, author, and newsletter publisher. After emigrating to Canada in 1967, at the age of twenty, Satin co-founded the Toronto Anti-Draft Programme, which helped bring American Vietnam War resisters to Canada. In 1968 he wrote the *Manual for Draft-Age Immigrants to Canada*, which had numerous print runs totalling an estimated 100,000 copies. Satin is also the author of *New Age Politics: Healing Self and Society*, and wrote the monthly political newsletters *New Options* (1983–1992) and *Radical Middle* (1998–2009). His most recent book is *New Age Politics: Our Only Real Alternative* (40th Anniversary Edition).

IT IS STILL RELATIVELY EASY FOR DRAFT-AGE AMERICANS — and in fact, all Americans — to immigrate to Canada. One informative website is sponsored by the Government of Canada, and can be accessed by typing the phrase "Apply to immigrate to Canada" into your search engine, or by entering the URL http://www.cic.gc.ca/english/immigrate/apply.asp. Another helpful site is sponsored by the Campbell Cohen law firm and can be accessed by typing "US Citizens Moving to Canada — NAFTA" or entering http://www.canadavisa.com/canada-immigration-usa-citizens.html.

Deserters from the U.S. military may have a more difficult time than they did during the Vietnam War; they may wish to consult the Toronto-based War Resisters Support Campaign website, http://resisters.ca, and peruse Sarah Hipworth and Luke Stewart's book *Let Them Stay: U.S. War Resisters in Canada, 2004–2016*, published in Canada.

The A List

Passing Ceremony Helen Weinzweig

Mermaids and Ikons Gwendolyn MacEwan

The Bush Garden Northrop Frye

Made for Happiness Jean Vanier

Hard Core Logo Nick Craine

The Big Why Michael Winter

The Little Girl Who Was Too Fond of Matches Gaetan Soucy

Death Goes Better with Coca-Cola Dave Godfrey

Basic Black with Pearls Helen Weinzweig

Ticknor Sheila Heti

This All Happened Michael Winter

Kamouraska Anne Hebert

The Circle Game Margaret Atwood

De Niro's Game Rawi Hage

Eleven Canadian Novelists Interviewed by Graeme Gibson

Like This Leo McKay Jr.

The Honeyman Festival Marian Engel

La Guerre Trilogy Roch Carrier

Selected Poems Alden Nowlan

No Pain Like This Body Harold Sonny Ladoo

Poems for all the Annettes Al Purdy

Five Legs Graeme Gibson

Selected Short Fiction of Lisa Moore

Survival Margaret Atwood

Queen Rat Lynn Crosbie

Ana Historic Daphne Mariatt

Civil Elegies Dennis Lee

The Outlander Gil Adamson

The Hockey Sweater and Other Stories Roch Carrier